TRAVELLERS

AUSTRIA

Written and updated by Brent Gregston
Original photography by Christopher Holt

Published by Thomas Cook Publishing
A division of Thomas Cook Tour Operations Limited.
Company registration no. 1450464 England
The Thomas Cook Business Park, Unit 9, Coningsby Road,
Peterborough PE3 8SB, United Kingdom
Email: books@thomascook.com, Tel: + 44 (0) 1733 416477
www.thomascookpublishing.com

Produced by Cambridge Publishing Management Limited
Burr Elm Court, Main Street, Caldecote CB23 7NU

ISBN: 978-1-84848-068-1

First edition © 2007 Thomas Cook Publishing
This second edition © 2009
Text © Thomas Cook Publishing
Maps © Thomas Cook Publishing/PCGraphics (UK) Limited
Transport map © Communicarta Limited

Series Editor: Maisie Fitzpatrick
Project Editor: Linda Bass
Production/DTP: Steven Collins

Printed and bound in Italy by Printer Trento

Cover photography: Front L–R: © Alan Copson City Pictures/Alamy;
© Jack Sullivan/Alamy; © International Photobank/Alamy
Back: © Thomas Cook

LONDON BOROUGH OF WANDSWORTH		
9030 00000 2660 4		
Askews		23-Apr-2009
914.3604 GREG		£9.99
		WWX0004434/0314

Although every care has been taken in compiling this publication, and the
contents are believed to be correct at the time of printing, Thomas Cook Tour
Operations Limited cannot accept any responsibility for errors or omissions,
however caused, or for changes in details given in the guidebook, or for the
consequences of any reliance on the information provided. Descriptions and
assessments are based on the author's views and experiences when writing and
do not necessarily represent those of Thomas Cook Tour Operations Limited.

The paper used for this book has been independently certified as having
been sourced from well-managed forests and other controlled sources
according to the rules of the Forest Stewardship Council.
This book has been printed and bound in Italy by Printer Trento S.r.l.,
an FSC certified company for printing books on FSC mixed paper in
compliance with the chain of custody and on products labelling standards.

FSC
Mixed Sources
Product group from well-managed
forests and other controlled sources
Cert no. CQ-COC-000012
www.fsc.org
© 1996 Forest Stewardship Council

Contents

Introduction

Austria needs no introduction. The country has been famous for its Alpine scenery since Europeans learned to love the Alps in the 18th century and the tourist industry was born. Yet the reality behind the travel posters is interesting, now more than ever. With the admission of ten more countries to the European Union (EU) in May 2004, Austria moved back into the heart of Europe. Vienna, once the capital of a vast multinational empire, is now a melting pot and epicentre of the newly emerging central Europe.

In Austria, great natural beauty and landmarks of European culture are strangely compressed. A blind turn can lead through a medieval gatehouse or into an ice age valley. No matter how often you look at the map, there will be unexpected encounters: a mountain lake with 25°C (77°F) water or a roadside chapel painted by a wandering Venetian 400 years ago. Scattered throughout the country are palaces, abbeys, splendid

A Salzburg marionette

churches, forbidding castles and historic residences. Spectacular high-altitude roads in the Alps mean that you can cross the world's non-tropical vegetation and climate zones in the space of an afternoon. Austria is deeply Roman Catholic and, at times, the calendar seems to be a succession of holidays and festivals. Depending on when and where you pull off the road, you can find yourself in the middle of the National Day speech of a Tyrolean mayor, listening to a priest pray over a loudspeaker during a Corpus Christi procession, or raising a glass at a Danube wine festival.

The country known for composers like Schubert and Mozart has always had a knack for juggling serious high culture with its contemporary alternatives. Salzburg may specialise in the music of its native son Mozart, but there are musicians in the street as well as in the concert hall, and the most popular opera performances are given by marionettes.

Natural History Museum, Vienna

The land

The Republik Österreich (Eastern Empire), or just Österreich, is small and predominantly mountainous but stretches almost 600km (373 miles) from the Austrian Alps in the west to the Danube Basin in the east. It is pear-shaped with a narrow corridor of land in the west that separates Germany from Italy by a mere 32–60km (20–37 miles) and, in the east, it has a north–south width of 280km (174 miles).

Geography

The Alps cover 62 per cent of Austria. The central Alps include areas that are permanently glaciated such as the Ötztal Alps on the Tyrolean Italian border and the Hohe Tauern in eastern Tyrol and Carinthia. At 3,798m (12,461ft), the Grossglockner in the province of Carinthia is the highest mountain in Austria.

Austria is located in the central European Temperate Zone, but the presence of the Alps creates the widest range of climatic zones and the chance to hop between climates. In summer, for instance, you can ski on a glacier and then descend to a valley for a lake swim. Winters and summers vary dramatically from year to year. Sometimes the lower ski resorts (including Kitzbühel) run out of snow early, and a warm summer can make you think you are in Italy.

The River Danube in the Wachau

Vineyards cover huge areas around Neusiedl

Human geography

Austria is one of the least densely populated states of Western and central Europe because of the Alps, with only 93 inhabitants per square kilometre. Over 90 per cent of the population are ethnic Austrian, and 4 per cent are Serbs, Croats and Slovenes. Three out of four Austrians are Catholic, and one in 20 is Muslim. Austria has an ageing population – the average age is 40.

The *Föhn* is a hot, dry wind that blows in the spring and autumn, bringing with it clear weather and intense blue skies. It has a reputation for making people moody. Scientists have never established a definitive cause-and-effect relationship, but the *Föhn* remains a socially acceptable excuse for being grumpy.

Cities

A quarter of all Austrians (2 million) live in or near Vienna. Graz is the second largest city, followed by Innsbruck, Linz and Salzburg.

Economy

Austria has one of the highest gross domestic products (GDPs) in Europe. Big money-making sectors include tourism, banking and forestry.

The demise of the Iron Curtain opened new investment opportunities in Eastern Europe.

Size

The Republic of Austria is just slightly larger than Maine in the US, or Scotland. Its total area is 83,870sq km (32,382 sq miles).

City
Large Town
Small Town
Border
Motorway
Main Road
Minor Road
Airport
Railway

0   50km
0   25 miles

Nuremberg

A9

Regensburg

A3

Stuttgart

Danube   GERMANY   Landshut

Ulm   Augsburg

Munich

A96

Franz Josef Strauss

Braunau am Inn

A7   A8

Salzburg

A96   WA Mozart

Bregenz   Kufstein   Hallein

Kitzbühel

Feldkirch   A12   Schwaz

LIECHTENSTEIN   Landeck   Innsbruck   Bad Gastein

VADUZ   Bludenz   A13   Grossvenediger   3360   Grossglockner   3798

Chur

SWITZERLAND   Lienz

Bolzano

ITALY

A22   A23

N   Trento   Udine

A27

History

44–9 million years ago	The Alps rise up above the floor of the vast Tethys Sea.
30,000 years ago	Stone Age people live in the cave of Tischoferhöhle near the Kaiser Mountains in the Tyrol.
2000–700 BC	The Celts give the Alps their name (Celtic for 'mountains' or 'high places').
15 BC–AD 500	The Romans occupy Austria and create the provinces of Noricum and Raetia.
AD 550	After the fall of the Roman Empire, the Germanic tribes of Bajuwaren (i.e. Bavarians) and Alemannen invade Austria.
1273	An Austrian noble from the Habsburg family is elected Holy Roman Emperor.
1493	Maximilian I becomes Holy Roman Emperor and makes Innsbruck the centre of his European empire.

The Austrian Alps

1519	Charles V (reigned 1519–56), Maximilian's grandson, rules over Austria, Germany, the Low Countries, parts of Italy, Spain and parts of the New World.
1529	The Turks besiege Vienna, beginning almost two centuries of conflict. Austria eventually gains possession of Hungary.
1556	Charles V retires to a monastery, splitting his kingdom between his son (King Philip II of Spain) and brother (Ferdinand I of Austria).
1683	The Turks besiege and nearly capture Vienna. They are driven off. Vienna's first coffee house opens.
1805	Napoleon defeats Austria at Austerlitz and forces Holy Roman Emperor Franz II to hand over the imperial crown. Napoleon marries Franz II's daughter, Marie-Louise.
1815	The Congress of Vienna takes place.

Vienna's coffee house tradition dates back to the 1600s

1816	Salzburg becomes part of Austria.
1866	Prussia defeats Austria and excludes it from involvement in the modern German nation.
1914	Austria fires the first shots of World War I to avenge the assassination of the heir to the Habsburg throne.
1919	After its defeat in World War I, the Austro-Hungarian Empire is divided into separate democratic nations. Austria becomes a small, landlocked country.

1921 Adolf Hitler (1889–1945), an Austrian by birth, takes charge of the National Socialist German Workers' Party.

1938–45 German troops march into Austria on 11 March 1938 and meet no resistance. It becomes part of the German Reich. Austrians serve in the German army between 1939 and 1945. Apart from Hitler himself, other Austrians, such as Ernst Kaltenbrunner, play a prominent role in the Holocaust. The concentration camps at Mauthausen and Gusen were among the worst in the Third Reich.

1945–55 Allied and Soviet troops occupy Austria. When they withdraw, Austria is one of Europe's poorer countries. Within a little more than a generation, it will enter the ranks of the ten richest countries in the world.

1964 & 1976 Innsbruck hosts the Winter Olympics twice in 12 years.

1987 The US places Austrian President Kurt Waldheim on its watch list of 'subversives, terrorists and criminals' because of his Nazi past.

1995 Austria becomes a member of the EU.

2000 The far-right Freedom Party (FPÖ) gains seats in Austria's parliament by campaigning under the slogan 'Überfremdung' (Too many foreigners). It also draws on widespread disillusionment with the corruption of the two main political parties.

2004 Heinz Fischer, a centre-left politician, is elected president. Austrian-born Arnold Schwarzenegger is elected governor of California.

2006 'Mozartmania' grips Austria as the country celebrates the 250th anniversary of his birth.

2008 Along with Switzerland, Austria hosts the UEFA Euro football tournament.

2009 The 200th anniversary of Joseph Haydn's death is commemorated by various exhibitions and concerts throughout the year.

The Belvedere Palace in Vienna, built when the Austrian Empire was at its peak

Politics

At the beginning of the 21st century, Austria's Second Republic is a stable federal republic with a written constitution based on the principles of representative democracy and the rule of law. Austria has opted for a federal government structure. Nine Federal Provinces divide Austria along geographical and cultural lines: Vienna, Upper Austria (Oberösterreich), Burgenland, Lower Austria (Niederösterreich), Styria (Steiermark), Carinthia (Kärtnen), Salzburg, Tyrol and Vorarlberg.

Austria today is a small but prosperous remnant of the Austro-Hungarian Empire that ceased to exist in 1918. Attempts to establish a stable democracy in the interwar years failed, and the country embraced National Socialist totalitarianism in 1938. Following the defeat of National Socialism in 1945, however, Austria

Vienna's parliament

began again to move step by step towards democracy.

After the Iron Curtain went up in 1948, Vienna became a haven for refugees fleeing the Hungarian Revolution of 1956, the failed Prague Spring of 1968, and the persecution of Jews in the Soviet Union. In the summer of 1989, Foreign Minister Alois Mock of Austria and his Communist Hungarian counterpart Gyula Horn cut through the barbed wire along a lonely border post dividing Western and Eastern Europe. The act was not just symbolic: 700 East Germans reached the West without being shot. This breach would ultimately allow tens of thousands of East Germans to leave the country and contribute to the fall of the Berlin Wall and the end of the Cold War.

Since Austria's admittance into the EU in 1995, the federal government has begun ceding core responsibilities to supranational institutions at an increasing rate. However, Austria's relations with the EU hit a low point

The spires of the town hall in Vienna

when the far-right Freedom Party (FPÖ) was invited to form a coalition government in 2000. The party's leader until 2005, Jörg Haider, was the son of a Nazi official and given to praising the 'good side' of the Nazi regime. His electoral success was based on an appeal to 'Austria for the Austrians' and on widespread disillusionment with the corruption of the two main political parties. The 14 other EU member states reacted by imposing diplomatic sanctions. However, relations were normalised after an independent EU report concluded that violence against foreigners 'had been less frequent in Austria than in many other countries of the EU'. Two years later, the FPÖ did poorly in elections.

In 2006, the Green Party achieved their best ever result, winning 21 seats in parliament in an election where ecology was the subject of intense debate, and confirming the importance of green issues in Austria, which now derives 20 per cent of its energy from renewable sources.

In July 2008, the government's coalition of the two main political parties collapsed only 18 months after it was formed. Elections were held in September, with strong gains for the far-right parties.

Culture

Austria has a fixation with Kultur (culture). The emperors, kings, princes, prince-bishops and dukes who wielded power through the centuries created a vast Kulturgut – a cultural heritage. Even small towns will sometimes astonish visitors with their fabulous art collections. Post-war prosperity and major subsidies for the arts have nourished this tradition.

Beginnings

Despite five centuries of occupation and settlement by Romans, there are only a few interesting Roman ruins in Austria. These include Carnuntum, downstream from Vienna, Teurnia in Carinthia, and Aguntum near the town of Lienz (in Ost Tyrol). The first great building boom to leave a major mark on the country began in the 10th century with the erection of vaulted churches and the foundation of monasteries such as the one at Melk. The great door of the Stephansdom in Vienna also dates from this era.

Gothic and Renaissance

Hallenkirchen (Hall-churches) are characteristic of the late-Gothic style in Austria. Their nave and aisles are the same height and are only separated by pillars, as in Vienna's Augustinerkirche and the Stephansdom. In general, late Gothic architecture remained resolutely sober – there was no flamboyant style, as in France. However, Gothic painting and sculpture underwent a sea change. The suffering of Christ was portrayed in ever more human terms, for instance in the great altarpiece by Michael Pacher in St Wolfgang.

The influence of the Renaissance was weak in Austria, with a few notable exceptions such as the city of Salzburg. Here, the prince-archbishops tried to build a 'new Rome' at the foot of the Alps. The most important examples of Renaissance sculpture are the figures surrounding the tomb of Maximilian I in Innsbruck.

Baroque and rococo

Beginning in the middle of the 17th century, the Baroque style swept everything before it, setting off a building boom and keeping the interior decorators busy. Any community with money invested in lavish Baroque facelifts of existing Gothic or Romanesque churches. The Baroque style is passionate, sensual and theatrical. In Baroque palaces, mirrors were used to create an illusion of infinity. Salzburg's Kollegienkirche, by Johann Bernhard Fischer Erlach (1656–1723), was a ground-breaking achievement. The rococo style pushed the decorative elements of Baroque to their stagiest limit, adding garlands, medallions and vegetation. In Austria, rococo was called 'Maria-Theresa Baroque'.

Neoclassicism and *Jugendstil*

After the waning of rococo, there was a severe swing of the pendulum. A sober style, neoclassicism relies heavily on columns and pediments.

In 1887, a group of dissatisfied Viennese artists, headed by Gustav Klimt, broke with the conservative Academy of Fine Arts to promote the radically new kind of art known as *Jugendstil*, inspired by the organic, fluid designs of Art Nouveau and the more geometric designs of the English Arts and Crafts movement. This Association of Visual Artists Vienna Secession presented its first exhibition in 1898, the same year the new Secession building was completed. This building is considered to be Europe's first example of 20th-century architecture.

Startling architectural detail in Vienna

Heimat

Heimat is usually translated as 'home' or 'homeland', but the word also conveys a sense of rural or provincial belonging. *Heimat*, in contrast to *Kultur* (culture), is about the life of mountain farmers, miners, cheese-makers, metalworkers, glass-blowers and hunters. *Heimat* recalls the days when the Alps were impassable and there existed many distinct Alpine subcultures. The inhabitants of one valley often had their own dialect, dress, architecture and folklore, and these differences distinguished them from the people in the next valley. Prosperity, tourism and television have greatly eroded these traditions, but you can get a feel for Alpine folklore by visiting a *Heimatmuseum* and looking at traditional furniture,

A typical mountain village in Ötztal

costumes, farm tools, carnival masks and Christmas Nativity scenes.

There are also open-air museums where wooden buildings have been collected from all over Austria to show different styles of vernacular architecture. The people living in the mountains were usually desperate to make ends meet and displayed great ingenuity in creating things for their own use – cultivating flax, forging spoons, painting hope chests – and in selling things to the outside world. Many ultimately became itinerant, peddling canaries, hawking snake oil, and yodelling for strangers.

Traditional dress depicted in a mural

Folk music

Austria has a venerable folk music tradition. Music groups from the Tyrol's Ziller Valley sang and yodelled their way all over Europe in the 19th century, appearing before the British royal family and the Russian Czar. We have one of these groups, the Rainer Truppe, to thank for the popularity of *Silent Night*. Unfortunately, folk music is often misrepresented in kitschy, made-for-tourist shows. Traditionally, yodelling was not only humorous but it was used to express all kinds of emotions, at a wedding or a funeral. The chances of hearing authentic Alpine music are much better if local groups (*Gesangsverein* or *Volksbildungswerk*) are involved and

the performance takes place in a community hall rather than a hotel.

Folk costumes

The people of Austria wear a remarkable range of *Trachten* (folk costumes), particularly on Sundays and holidays. The traditional garments vary in each region and town. There was a time when, if you knew what to look for, you could tell at a glance that a person wearing *Tracht* was married or single, a hunter or a farmer, living in the mountains or in a town. *Trachten* are labours of love that require countless hours of sewing and stitching to make. Many elements are hand-embroidered, and painstaking attention is given to feathers, colours, buttons (made of silver or horn) and fabrics.

Festivals and events

The Austrian calendar is full of festivals – local, patriotic and religious. They often involve processions, dressing up in Trachten *(folk costumes) and much eating and drinking. Some of the seasonal festivals in the region, although adapted to Christianity, have their roots in pagan ritual.*

January/February

Fasching (**carnival**) celebrations can begin as early as January, but the main events occur during the week leading up to Shrove Tuesday in February. There are costume parades, feasts and clowning. This is celebrated with particular enthusiasm in Vienna, Salzburg and Innsbruck. There are 'processions of ghosts' in Imst (*Schemenlaufen*, every four years), Telfs (*Schleicherlaufen*, every five years) and Nassereith (*Schellerlaufen*, every three years).

March/April

Palm Sunday processions

May/June

1–2 May **Gauderfest** is in Zell am Ziller, Tyrol. Lederhosen-clad men engage in epic events like finger-wrestling, hoisting crates of beer-steins or snuff-sniffing.
15 June **Corpus Christi** processions.

July/August

Schützen and **Feuerwehrfeste** in the Tyrol (militia and fire department festivities).

September/October

Viehscheid or **Almabtrieb** is an autumn cattle-drive from the high Alpine pastures. It is celebrated all over the Alps, particularly in Pfunds and St Johann in Tyrol.
Wine festivals take place in the wine villages of the Danube Valley, Styria and Burgenland.

November/December

St Martin's Day Children pass by people's doors with paper lanterns and candles, and sing songs in return for a treat (somewhat like the American Hallowe'en), followed by a traditional goose dinner.
Christkindlmarkt (Christmas markets) are common throughout the region during Advent. The markets are set up in front of cathedrals, and brass bands

and choirs play carols. You can shop for handmade gifts such as tree ornaments made of wood and straw, or woollen goods. You can also mix with locals who ignore the cold and stand around eating *Bratwurst* or *Reiberdatschi* (potato pancakes) and drinking *Glühwein* (hot wine mixed with spices and, on request, rum). Most churches have concerts leading up to and on Christmas Day.

Krippen (Christmas Nativity scenes) are displayed in many villages and towns.

Public holidays

1 Jan – New Year's Day (Neujahr)
6 Jan – Epiphany (Heilige Drei Könige)
Mar/Apr, date changes annually – Easter Monday (Ostermontag)

1 May – Labour Day (Maifeiertag)
May, date changes annually – Ascension Day (Christi Himmelfahrt)
May/June, date changes annually – Whit Monday (Pfingstmontag)
June, date changes annually – Corpus Christi (Fronleichnahm)
15 Aug – Feast of the Assumption (Mariä Himmelfahrt)
26 Oct – National Day (Nationalfeiertag), anniversary of the declaration of neutrality
1 Nov – All Saints' Day (Allerheiligen)
8 Dec – Immaculate Conception (Maria Empfängnis)
25 Dec – Christmas Day (Erster Weihnachtstag)
26 Dec – Feast of St Stephen (Stephanstag).

Wine festivals in Burgenland celebrate the local crop

Festivals and events

Highlights

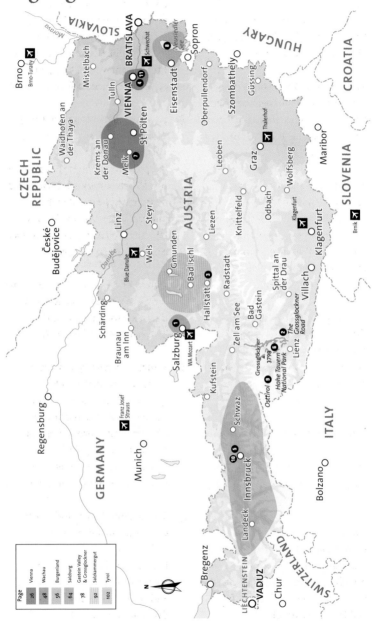

Page	
26	Vienna
48	Wachau
56	Burgenland
64	Salzburg
78	Gastein Valley & Grossglockner
92	Salzkammergut
102	Tyrol

❶ Festung Hohensalzburg Central Europe's biggest castle, built and rebuilt for 600 years, broods over Salzburg, the historic city that gave birth to Mozart (*see p66*).

❷ The Grossglockner Road Europe's grandest mountain highway offers panoramic Alpine views and a parking place near Austria's highest peak (*see p82*).

❸ Hallstatt A period of human history – the Hallstatt Age – is named after this mysterious lakeside village and its Celtic necropolis. The magical Dachstein Ice Caves are just a few minutes away (*see p94*).

❹ Hofburg The Habsburgs ruled their empire from this palace for six centuries. It is home to great art collections, dancing Lipizzaner horses, Austria's largest library and the Vienna Boys' Choir (*see p30*).

❺ Hofkirche in Innsbruck Europe's most famous tomb was created by an unprecedented team of artists, sculptors and metalworkers during half a century (*see p105*).

❻ Hohe Tauern National Park Europe's largest national park is a realm of pristine Alpine pastures, vast forests and glacial formations, and a refuge for flora and fauna (*see p122*).

❼ Melk The famous Benedictine abbey is one of Europe's most splendid examples of Baroque architecture. The monastery contains one of the world's finest libraries and a wealth of paintings, tapestries and art objects (*see p50*).

❽ Neusiedler See (Neusiedl Lake) The mysterious steppe lake on the Hungarian border – it has disappeared and reappeared several times in its history – is surrounded by rolling hills dotted with vineyards, spas and castles. The lake has gained worldwide fame as a bird sanctuary (*see p61*).

❾ Osttirol East Tyrol's remote Alpine valleys, each one more idyllic than the last, harbour unspoiled Tyrolean villages (*see p119*).

❿ Schloss Ambras Tyrol's largest castle presents the formidable spectacle of jousting mannequins and medieval arms and armour. The Renaissance Spanischer Saal (Spanish Room) is filled with frescoes of Tyrolean nobility and Habsburg family portraits (*see p107*).

⓫ Schönbrunn Palace and Garden One of the highlights of Baroque architecture in Europe, the palace has changed little since it was commissioned by Maria Theresa and completed in the year of her death in 1780 (*see p45*).

Suggested itineraries

Weekend trips
Burgenland

Explore Eisenstadt, capital of
Burgenland province, beginning with
Schloss Esterházy. Haydn's house, now a
museum, is open to visitors, and he is
buried in the Bergkirche above the
town. Stop in the St Margarethen stone
quarry to see artists of different
nationalities at work, or attend (in
summer) a performance of the Passion
Play. Walk among Renaissance and
Baroque houses in Rust with storks'
nests on their roofs. In the little town of
Neusiedl, stroll out on the Neusiedl
Lake causeway.

Salzburg

Explore the Altstadt (Old Town),
which is densely packed with churches,
palaces, museums, fountains and shops.
Take the funicular up to Festung
Hohensalzburg to see the museum,
and attend a concert in the Golden
Hall. Contemplate the Austrian
fascination with death at St Peter's,
one of the oldest and most beautiful
cemeteries in the world.

Long weekends
Danube

Travel between Vienna and Salzburg via
the Danube Valley. Take a cruise from

Joseph Haydn's piano at the Haydn Haus, Eisenstadt

Krems to Melk, and cycle back along the most popular riverside bike path in Europe, through gentle valleys, wine villages and majestic monasteries.

Grossglockner Road

The high Alpine road can be combined with the Felbertauernstrasse (B108) to create one long circular route. This traverses the Hohe Tauern National Park, passes through a classic *Almlandschaft* (mountain farmscape) with awe-inspiring views of the jagged Dolomites, and penetrates the *Bergwelt* (mountain world) of East Tyrol (Osttirol).

Ötz Valley

Cruise the Ötztal and its side valleys, getting out of the car now and again to admire a landscape formed by cataclysmic landslides at the end of the last ice age. Visit Stuiben Waterfall, the highest in the Tyrol, and the tiny hamlet of Rofenhöfe (2,014m/6,608ft), the highest village in Austria that is inhabited year round.

Vienna

Follow the Ringstrasse, the boulevard that bounds the historic heart of Vienna. Save a day for museums and the Hofburg (Imperial Palace) and half a day for the Schönbrunn Palace. Spend an evening at the opera and another in the Museum Quarter, where DJs spin tunes in the courtyard surrounded by modern art.

One-week trips
Kitzbühel and Ziller valleys, Krimml Waterfalls

Complete the circuit of Kitzbühel and Ziller valleys, with an excursion into Salzburg province to stand at the foot of the Krimml Waterfalls, Europe's highest. Take the spectacular cable car from Zell am See or the Penkenbahn gondola from Mayrhofen into the Zillertal Alps. Drive the mountain toll road to Hirschbichlalm. Escape the tourist masses in the high mountain valley of Wildschönau in the heart of the Kitzbüheler Alps.

Innsbruck and the Lower Inn Valley

Visit Innsbruck, Kufstein Fortress, Rattenberg, the historic centre of Hall and the Open-air Museum in Kramsach. Take the cogwheel train up to Achensee. Walk through the cave-like Wolfsklamm (gorge) that leads to the monastery of St Georgenberg. Drive up the Alpbach Valley to Alpbach village, the most beautiful, according to Austrian opinion polls, in the country.

Salzkammer lakes

Visit Salzburg and then cruise the fjord-like scenery of turquoise lakes, and the historic villages like Hallstatt. Spend a couple of nights in a small historic town such as Gmunden or Bad Ischl. Use the alternative forms of transportation when possible: 19th-century ferry boats, puffing historic trains, and dizzying cable-car hoists to Alpine summits.

Vienna

Behind its stately façades, Vienna (Wien in German) has always been a city with more than its share of contradictions. As the imperial capital of an atavistic empire, Vienna gave birth to modern architecture, atonal music and psychoanalysis.

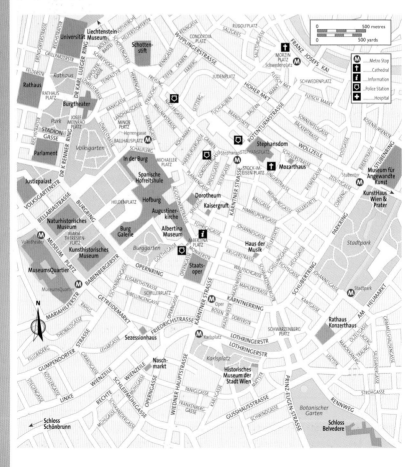

Carved figures on the front of the town hall

Vienna is one of Europe's most liveable mid-size cities, yet in cultural terms it is a superpower endowed by its Habsburg emperors with seemingly limitless artistic treasures – the Habsburg Empire stretched from South America to Eastern Europe. Much of the world's greatest classical music was composed within Vienna's city limits.

The Cold War relegated the Austrian capital to the fringes of Europe, but with the fall of the Iron Curtain, Vienna has moved to centre stage again. To get a feel for Vienna today, simply visit the Museum Quarter, one of the world's largest and most popular contemporary art venues, rivalling New York's Metropolitan Museum of Art and the Pompidou in Paris. Architecturally, beyond the Gothic towers, Baroque domes and 19th-century mansions of Vienna's inner city, an ultramodern skyline has formed, created by Europe's leading architects.

If the Viennese show signs of breaking free from the past, it doesn't stop them from learning how to waltz and gathering in centuries-old coffee houses. Even if you are not writing poetry or plotting revolution, there is still no better place to remake the world or to contemplate the city, with its many contradictions, than in a coffee house. For the price of a single cup of coffee, you can sit all day long in any of Vienna's classic cafés – each one has its own history and unique character – and still be treated like a king.

Albertina Museum

These former state rooms on the south end of the Hofburg (*see p30*) are filled with one of the world's greatest graphic

The Albertina Museum was renovated in 2003

art collections. Founded in 1776 by Duke Albert of Saxe-Teschen, it contains a mind-boggling 900,000 prints and 60,000 drawings by most of the great Western artists of the last six centuries. Badly damaged in World War II and sadly neglected for years afterwards, the neoclassical palace was given a massive facelift in 2003. With ten times more gallery space, the Albertina can now run three simultaneous temporary exhibitions – especially important since the works on paper can only be displayed for a short time because of their sensitivity to light. The museum also owns an architecture collection and a newly created collection of photographs (Helmut Newton and Lisette Model, among others).

Albertinaplatz 1. Tel: 534 83 0. www.albertina.at. Open: 10am–6pm, Wed 10am–9pm. Admission charge. U, bus: Karlsplatz/Oper.

Augustinerkirche

Erected in the early 1300s, this was the family church of the Habsburg imperial family. Perhaps the most striking tomb is that of Archduchess Maria Christine. Her grieving husband commissioned Antonio Canova to sculpt it between 1798 and 1805. According to a tradition that lasted from 1654 to 1878, the hearts (54 in all) of the Habsburgs were entombed in silver urns in a special vault, the *Herzgruft* (Burial Vault of the Hearts of the Habsburgs). The Gothic St George's Chapel (*access through the Loreto Chapel*) was where the Knights of the Order of St George once met. Franz Schubert conducted his *Mass* in F Major here, and Anton Bruckner premiered his *Mass* in F minor. The church has seen its share of weddings, too: Napoleon wed the Austrian Princess Marie Louise here in 1810 and Emperor Franz Joseph I made the beautiful 'Sissy' his Empress in 1854. *Augustinerstrasse 3. www.augustinerkirche. at (German only). Open: outside of High Mass, Sun & holidays 11am (except 10 July–23 Aug). Burial Vault of the Hearts of the Habsburgs. Open: visits by appointment only & Sun after High Mass (around 12.30pm). Free admission. U, bus: Karlsplatz/Oper.*

Haus der Musik

Dorotheum

Behind the Dorotheum's neoclassical façade is central Europe's largest auction house, established in 1707. Furniture, porcelain and jewellery from various centuries are auctioned here. The objects are first exhibited in one room, and sold in another. It is an attraction for Viennese and tourists alike. *Dorotheergasse 17. Tel: 515 60 0. www.dorotheum.com. Open: weekdays 9am–6pm, Sat 9am–5pm. Closed: Sun. Free admission.*

Haus der Musik (House of Music)

The world of music and sound is presented on six floors in this award-winning museum. The most popular exhibit allows you to compose your own waltzes electronically and conduct them virtually with the Vienna Philharmonic on a big screen. A free English-language audio tape explains the exhibits. *Seilerstätte 30. Tel: 516 48. www.hdm.at. Open: 10am–10pm. Admission charge.*

Historisches Museum der Stadt Wien (Vienna Museum)

Three storeys of art and history tell the story of Vienna from the Neolithic Age to the mid-20th century. Highlights include archaeological finds from the Roman legionary camp of Vindobona, original stained-glass windows and sculptures from St Stephen's Cathedral, and 'Turkish Plunder' from the siege of Vienna in 1683. The 19th-century collection gives a complete overview

Exhibits in the Treasury at the Hofburg

of the Biedermeier period, and there are works by the famous Wiener Werkstätte, as well as the reconstructed apartment of architect Adolf Loos. *Karlsplatz 4. Tel: 505 87 47. www.wienmuseum.at. Open: 9am–6pm. Closed: Mon. Admission charge, free on Sun for permanent exhibition. U, bus: Karlsplatz/Oper.*

Hofburg (Imperial Palace)

If a single building can encapsulate the centuries of Habsburg rule, it is the Hofburg, home to the imperial rulers from the 13th century. While its origins are medieval, the palace was continually rebuilt and expanded throughout the long history of the Habsburg Empire. Only a small number of its 2,500 rooms are open to the public. Enter through St

Michael's Gate (*just off Michaelerplatz*) to tour the lavish Kaiserapparments (Imperial Apartments). The first six rooms are devoted to the life of Empress 'Sissy' Elisabeth (1837–98). The one-way route leads through more royal rooms, including the study and bedroom of Emperor Franz Joseph and Sissy's Great Salon. You have to exit the palace and re-enter through In der Burg (Palace Square) to tour the 16 rooms of the Hofburg's Schatzkammer (Treasury). Here, you can gaze on the jewels that symbolised the might and dignity of the imperial house for centuries: the imperial crown of the Holy Roman Empire, the crown of Emperor Rudolf II (1552–1612), the coronation mantle of King Roger II of Sicily, an array of swords, medals and reliquaries all encrusted with jewels, and, of course, the orb and sceptre.

The Neue Burg (New Palace) was built for heir apparent Franz Ferdinand (*enter through Heldenplatz/Heroes' Square*). He would have lived here had he not been assassinated at Sarajevo in 1914. The palace was part of a grandiose plan at the beginning of the 20th century to expand the imperial headquarters in keeping with Austro-Hungary's superpower status. World War I and the monarchy's fall in 1918 put an end to all that. The palace houses three museums that form part of a complex with the Kunsthistorisches Museum (*same ticket, see p33*): an armoury, a collection of historical musical instruments, and classical statuary from Ephesus.

The Hofburg is also home to the famous Spanish Riding School and its prancing Lipizzaner horses (*see www.srs.at*). The riders perform equestrian ballet to classical music beneath chandeliers in a Baroque arena.

The Vienna Boys' Choir (*www.wsk.at*) can be heard in the Hofburg Chapel celebrating Sunday Mass throughout winter and spring, and in occasional concerts on other days.
Kaiserappartments. Tel: 533 75 70. www.hofburg-wien.at. Open: Sept–June 9am–5pm (ticket office closes 4.30pm); July & Aug 9am–5.30pm (ticket office closes 5pm). Admission charge. Schatzkammer. Tel: 525 24 0. www.khm.at. Open: 10am–6pm.

Closed: Tue. Admission charge. Neue Burg Museums. Tel: 525 24 48 4. www.khm.at. Open: 10am–6pm. Closed: Tue. Admission charge.

Kaisergruft (Imperial Burial Vault)

Since 1633, the Habsburg emperors, empresses, kings and queens have been buried (with one exception) in a crypt under the Capuchin church: 146 members of the ruling dynasty, including 12 emperors and 19 empresses and queens, have found their last resting place here. Not all Habsburgs were buried equal. The glorious double casket of Maria Theresa and husband Emperor Francis I is a stark contrast to the simple coffin of Joseph II. Franz Joseph, in 1916, was the last emperor entombed here. In 1989, a solemn funeral was held for Empress Zita, the widow of Emperor Charles I, who had reigned from 1916 to 1918. To this day, the Capuchin friars are the guardians and caretakers of the vault.
Tegetthoffstrasse. Tel: 512 68 53. www.kaisergruft.at (German only). Open: 10am–6pm. Admission charge. Bus: Karlsplatz/Oper; U1 & U3: Stephansplatz.

KunstHausWien

Once the bentwood factory Thonet, this building was remodelled by painter, sculptor and architect Friedensreich Hundertwasser (1928–2000). The KunstHausWien houses a permanent Hundertwasser exhibition on two floors, and two

Statues in front of the Kunsthistorisches Museum in Maria-Theresien-Platz

additional floors are devoted to changing exhibitions.

Not far away is the Hundertwasser-Haus (*at Löwengasse and Kegelgasse*). One of Vienna's most original buildings, it is a lived-in public housing complex. The floors undulate ('an uneven floor is a melody to the feet', according to Hundertwasser) and the roof is covered with earth and grass. There are large trees growing from inside the rooms, with limbs extending from the windows. Hundertwasser took no payment for the design, declaring that it was worth it, to 'prevent something ugly from going up in its place'.
Untere Weissgerberstrasse 13.
Tel: 712 04 91. www.kunsthauswien.com.
Open: 10am–7pm. Admission charge.
Tram 1: Radetzkyplatz.

Kunsthistorisches Museum

Rarely has a ruling family been as acquisitive or persistent in their art collecting as the Habsburgs. The result is one of the world's great art collections, amassed over a period of 600 years and housed in a grand building purpose-built in 1888. A few highlights: the largest Brueghel collection in the world, Raphael's *Madonna in the Meadow*, Vermeer's *The Allegory of Painting*, the Infanta paintings by Velazquez, as well as masterpieces by Caravaggio, Dürer, Rembrandt, Rubens, Titian and Tintoretto. The Collection of Sculpture and Decorative Arts is notable for Egyptian and Near Eastern

antiquities. Benvenuto Cellini's famous Salt-Cellar – it's been called the 'Mona Lisa of sculptures' (estimated value of 45 million euros) – was recovered in 2006 by tracing the mobile phone of the thief who demanded a 9 million euro reward for its return.
Maria-Theresien-Platz. Tel: 525 24 0.
www.khm.at. Tue–Sun 10am–6pm,
Thur 10am–9pm. Admission charge. U2:
MuseumsQuartier; U3: Volkstheater.

Liechtenstein Museum

In the final days of World War II, the fabulous Liechtenstein collections were carted to safety in Vaduz, the capital of the miniature principality. In 2004, the collection finally returned to its home in the Liechtenstein Garden Palace, itself a Baroque masterpiece in a rare state of preservation. The collection represents one of the largest collections of Rubens, and includes major works by Van Dyck, Lucas Cranach, Raphael and Rembrandt. These works are complemented by weaponry, porcelain and a large collection of bronzes.
Fürstengasse 1. Tel: 319 57 67 0.
www.liechtensteinmuseum.at.
Open: 10am–5pm. Closed: Wed & Thur.
Tram D, bus 40A: Bauernfeldplatz.
Admission charge.

Museum für Angewandte Kunst (Museum of Applied Art)

Founded as a showcase for national design, the museum consists of several cavernous galleries containing decorative objects and architectural

Museum für Angewandte Kunst

models from the turn of the 20th century. Pride of place goes to the Vienna Werkstätte pieces, including furniture by Josef Hoffmann, and paintings by Gustav Klimt. *Stubenring 5. Tel: 711 36 0. www.mak.at/e/jetzt/f_jetzt.htm. Open: Wed–Sun 10am–6pm, Tue 10am–midnight. Closed: Mon. Admission charge (admission free on Sat). U3, bus 74A: Stubentor.*

MuseumsQuartier (Museum Quarter)

Once the Habsburg imperial stables, the Museum Quarter is now a small city within a city. The equestrian buildings created by imperial architect Fischer von Erlach in the early 1700s have been converted to modern art galleries and cafés contained within ancient Baroque walls. More than just an exhibition centre, it has become a social and cultural around-the-clock happening for artists and young people (*coffee houses and dance clubs close at 4am*). In spring and summer, people gather by the thousands at pavement cafés in the courtyard without necessarily visiting the major museums. Two of Europe's newest and most important modern art museums both opened here in September 2001: the Museum of Modern Art (*www.mumok.at*)

The Museum of Modern Art in the Museum Quarter

and the Leopold Museum (*www.leopoldmuseum.org*); as well as Zoom Kindermuseum (a children's centre; *www.kindermuseum.at*). *Museumsplatz 1. Tel: 523 58 81. www.mqw.at. Open: 10am–7pm. U2: MuseumsQuartier; U3: Volkstheater.*

Naschmarkt

This market has the best of everything you can eat (Nasch means 'munchies'): fresh fruit and vegetables, fish, game, cases of wine, pyramids of eggs and forest mushrooms. Butchers compete to display the choicest cuts of meat and to sell the best *Würste* (sausages). The

Stock up at Naschmarkt

market covers an area where the Wien River flows underground, and it dates back to 1819. On Saturdays, it is also the site of a colourful flea market. *Rechte Wienzeile. Open: Mon–Fri 6am–6.30pm, Sat 6am–5pm.*

Prater

The Prater's Riesenrad is the Eiffel Tower of Ferris wheels. Along with Orson Welles, it steals the show in Carol Reed's 1949 thriller *The Third Man.* There are about 200 other attractions in the 'Wurstelprater' (Clown's Prater), as the Viennese call their amusement park, from shooting galleries, roller coasters, and ghost trains to bungee jumping and flight simulators. Children especially enjoy the merry-go-rounds, Punch and Judy shows and the old Viennese grotto train. There is also a 'Green Prater' – a former imperial hunting ground opened by Emperor Joseph II to the public. Today, it is appreciated by walkers, runners, cyclists and horse riders.

Open: depending on the time of year, 9am or 10am–8pm, 10pm or midnight. www.wienerriesenrad.at & www.prater.at. Admission charge. Tram D, U1: Praterstern.

Ringstrasse

Circling Vienna is the grand boulevard Ringstrasse, built to replace the medieval wall. A stroll around the Ringstrasse is arguably the best tour of Vienna; you can also take trams 1 and 2

(*Cont. on p45*)

The spires of the Votivkirche on the Ringstrasse

Walk: Vienna

Start in the square in front of Vienna's opera house, the Staatsoper – possibly the finest opera house in the world, lavishly subsidised and artistically demanding.

This walk may take half a day or a full day, depending on how many stops you make.

1 Staatsoper (State Opera)

The Staatsoper began its existence as the Imperial and Royal Court Opera, opening in May 1869 with a performance of Mozart's *Don Giovanni*. When Austria became a republic, 'Royal' was replaced by 'State'. World War II bombing all but destroyed the building, but it was reconstructed as closely to the original as possible and reopened in 1955 with Beethoven's *Fidelio*. The Staatsoper Museum (*Open: Tue–Sun 10am–6pm. Closed: Mon. Admission charge*), which opened at the end of 2005, tells the complete story.
Walk behind the opera house to Albertinaplatz.

2 Albertinaplatz

The square behind the opera is dominated by an equestrian statue of Archduke Albert – the pedestal was a former bastion of Vienna's fortifications. There is also the Danube fountain representing the rivers Danube and Wien. The 1988 *Monument against War and Fascism* on the north side marked the 50th anniversary of Austria's Nazi takeover. Its grey blocks were hewed in the quarry at the former Mauthausen concentration camp. The declaration of Austria's second republic is etched into one of the blocks. A sculpture depicts the hunched figure of a Jew being forced to wash the street with a brush after Austria was annexed by Hitler's Germany in 1938. Across the square are the Tourist Office and the Albertina Museum (*see pp27–8*).
Cross Albertinaplatz and enter Tegetthoffstrasse. Carry on one block towards the square, Neuer Markt. On the way, visit the Kaisergruft (see p31) and then cross Neuermarkt Square, turning left into Kärntner Strasse.

3 Kärntner Strasse

Kärntner Strasse is a window-shopper's paradise, with everything from hip department stores to couture classics and the most exquisite chocolates.

The Malteserkirche (Maltese Church) is a reminder that this was the route taken (southbound) by medieval crusaders. Just opposite is the Glaushaus Lobmeyr (*No 26*), a shop specialising in crystal chandeliers. The American bar in the Kärntner passage (*Durchgang*) was designed by Alfred Loos in 1908 with an interior of mahogany, leather, brass, marble and mirrors. The Casino Wien occupies the 17th-century Palais Esterházy.
At the end of Kärntner Strasse you come to Stephansplatz.

4 Stephansplatz

Stephansplatz is the pedestrian-only square surrounding Vienna's great Gothic cathedral. It's always filled with people, couples, families and teenagers, who gather below the ultramodern Haas Haus, the square's newest and most controversial building.
Take the street called Graben off Stephansplatz to the northwest.

5 Graben

Graben has a colourful history. It was a Roman moat (*Graben* means 'ditch'), medieval market and Baroque brothel. Although it is one of Vienna's richest streets – small family-run shops having made way for European chains like Zara and Hennes & Moritz – its most famous monument (the Pestsäule or Plague Pillar) dates from 1693. And its

Walk: Vienna

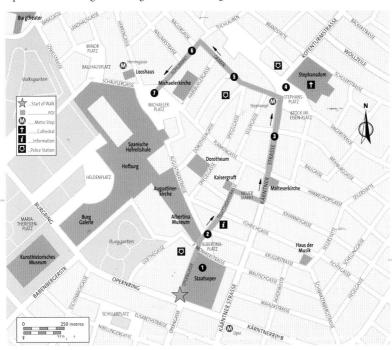

Boutiques on Kärntner Strasse

biggest tourist attraction is the public toilet, not just any lavatory, but the *Hausl*. Designed in 1905 by Secession-style architect Adolf Loos (he also designed the men's clothing store *No 13*), it is a splendid place of mosaics and marble.
Turn left into Kohlmarkt.

6 Kohlmarkt

Once a coal market, this street is now lined with some of the most expensive shops in Austria, including the Thonet furniture shop (*No 6*) and Demel (*No 14*) – Vienna's most famous chocolate shop specialising in Kandierte Veilchen (candied petals) and Katzenzungen (cat's tongues).

Alfred Loos designed the Manz bookshop (*No 16*), while the Secession-style Artariahaus (*No 9*) by Max Fabiani is regarded as an architectural prelude to the Looshaus (*see below*).
Continue on to Michaelerplatz.

7 Michaelerplatz

Much Viennese history is compressed into this single square. In the centre are the 2,000-year-old Roman ruins unearthed in 1992. Brazenly located just across from the Hofburg (Imperial Palace) is the famous corner building, the Looshaus (now occupied by a bank, the Raiffeisenbank). Designed in 1910, the structure was one of the first modern façades in Europe. The ageing Emperor Franz Joseph hated it so much that he ordered the palace shutters to be kept permanently closed. You can contemplate all this architectural history from the timeless Café Griensteidl (*No 2*). To turn your thoughts to the afterlife, step into Michaelerkirche (St Michael's Church), the former Court parish church where Mozart's prophetic, unfinished *Requiem* premiered in 1791. The crypt is full of neatly stacked bones, wooden caskets, several of them open, and mummies from the 17th and 18th centuries.

Michaelerplatz

The capital of music

Music is treated as one of the most important things in life in Vienna, just as it was in the days when Haydn, Mozart and Beethoven lived here, or, in a later generation, Brahms, Mahler, Bruckner and Richard Strauss.

The Mozart memorial at the Zentralfriedhof

Venerable venues

There are few evenings when you cannot attend an outstanding performance of a symphony, Lieder, string quartet or opera in Vienna. The season runs from 1 January to 30 June, reopening on 1 September. The Staatsoper (Vienna State Opera) is enormous and is the city's most prestigious music venue. The turn-of-the-20th-century Volksoper, focusing more on operetta, also embodies the Viennese love of music with less pretension and much lower prices. The Theater an der Wien dates back to 1801 – Beethoven's Fifth and Sixth symphonies were premiered here. Mahler and Strauss are said to have written music specifically for the perfect acoustics of the Musikverein's Goldene Saale (Golden Hall).

Composers' homes and tombs

Mozart's home in Vienna has been converted into the Mozarthaus Vienna, a centre dedicated to Mozart on four floors. Artefacts from the great composer's life, and the latest technology – opera by hologram – try to evoke what his life was like when he occupied the first-floor apartment and wrote *The Marriage of Figaro*

(*Domgasse 5. Tel: 512 17 91.
www.mozarthausvienna.at. Open:
10am–7pm. Admission charge*).

By comparison, the simple homes
of Schubert (*Nussdorfer Strasse 54*)
and Beethoven (the one in which he
composed *Eroica* is at
Döblingerhauptstrasse 92) are quite
modest. The Blue Danube House
(*Praterstrasse 54*) is where Strauss
composed the waltzes and polkas
that have kept the world dancing
ever since.

Some of the world's greatest
composers are buried in Vienna. You
can take a tram out to the
Zentralfriedhof (*Simmeringer
Hauptstrasse 232–244, district 11*), an
enormous cemetery where, in one
corner just beyond Gate 2, lie Brahms
and the Strauss family. Schubert, at
his request, lies beside Beethoven.
Also buried here are Salieri, Gluck and
Schönberg. In the centre of them all
stands a memorial to Mozart who
was buried in an unmarked grave.

MUSIC VENUES

Konzerthaus Lothringerstrasse 20.
Tel: 242 00 2. www.konzerthaus.at
Musikverein Bosendorferstrasse 12.
Tel: 505 81 90. www.musikverein.at
Theater an der Wien Linke Wienzeile 6.
Tel: 588 30 66 0. www.theater-wien.at
Vienna State Opera Opernring 2.
Tel: 514 44 22 50. www.wiener-staatsoper.at
Volksoper Währinger Strasse 78.
Tel: 514 44 36 70. www.volksoper.at

VIENNA MUSIC FESTIVALS

January–February
New Year's concert in the Goldene Saale of
the Musikverein.
The Viennese waltz, with hands linked and
bodies held close, is celebrated at more than
200 balls in the city.
Festival for early music in the Konzerthaus.

March–May
Osterklang (Easter Music Festival) in the
Theater an der Wien.
Spring Festival in the Konzerthaus.

May–June
Wiener Festwochen (Vienna International
Festival). *www.festwochen.at*
Every year orchestras from around the
world take part as the city's churches,
mansions and palaces host more than
150 different concerts.

July–September
KlangBogen Wien (Summer of Music
Festival) in the Theater an der Wien.
Rathausplatz Music Film Festival. Films
of concerts shown on big screen in front of
Vienna's City Hall.

October–November
Wien Modern (20th-century music) in the
Musikverein and Konzerthaus.
Schubertiade (last half of November) in
the Musikverein.

December
Mozartfest (first three weeks) in the
Konzerthaus.
New Year's Eve. Classical music is the
highlight of New Year's Eve in Vienna,
most notably the Vienna Philharmonic's
performance at Musikverein. The cathedral's
Purmerin bell rings in midnight, followed
by public performances of the Blue
Danube Waltz.

DER·ZEIT·IHRE·KVNST·
DER·KVNST·IHRE·FREIHEIT·

VER·SACRVM·

The Art Nouveau Sezessionhaus

or use the bike path. On the way, you pass the Hofburg Palace, City Hall, Parliament and Opera House. Opulent and pedestrianised Kärntner Strasse links the Ring with Stephansplatz. The architecture of the Ringstrasse, which dates from the latter half of the 19th century, is known as Eclecticism (or Historicism) because it consciously draws inspiration from the past. In other words, everything was built on the 'neo' principle. The Votivkirche is French neo-Gothic, Vienna's Rathaus (City Hall) is Flemish neo-Gothic, its parliament is Greek revival, the Vienna State Opera is French neo-Renaissance, the Museum of Applied Arts is Tuscan neo-Renaissance, and the Burgtheater (Court Theatre) displays a mixture of neo-Italian styles.

Schloss Belvedere
(Belvedere Palace)

One of the most exquisite Baroque structures in the world, the Belvedere represents the pomp and splendour of the Austrian Empire at the height of its power. The garden palace was built as a summer residence by Johann Lukas von Hildebrandt for Prince Eugene of Savoy (1663–1736), the brilliant military mind of his age. The palace houses the Austrian Gallery of the 19th and 20th centuries. The highlight for many is the large collection of Klimt paintings (including *The Kiss*). Also here are the prominent works of the French Impressionists, important paintings of the Viennese

Biedermeier era, and 20th-century works by Kokoschka and Hundertwasser, among others.
Prinz-Eugen-Strasse 27. Tel: 795 57 0. www.belvedere.at. Open: daily 10am–6pm (last admission 5.30pm). Admission charge.
Tram D: Schloss Belvedere.

Schloss Schönbrunn
(Schönbrunn Palace)

Schloss Schönbrunn is the Versailles of the Austro-Hungarian Empire. The former summer residence of the imperial Habsburgs, this Baroque palace has 1,400 rooms. The long line of illustrious occupants includes Empress Maria Theresa of Austria and Napoleon Bonaparte. Mozart gave his first concert – at the age of six – in the Mirror Room in 1762. The Napoleon Room is where Napoleon Bonaparte lived for six months. The 1815 Congress of Vienna convened in the opulent Great Gallery, lit by 4,000 candles. Emperor Franz Joseph was born here in 1830 and would reign an astonishing 68 years from 1848 to 1916. The monarch spent his last years entirely in the palace, which became the property of the new Republic of Austria only two years after his death. The palace is the second most popular tourist attraction in Vienna – the zoo in the palace grounds is the first – so you should get here early.
Schönbrunner Schlossstrasse 13. Tel: 811 10. www.schoenbrunn.at. Open: Apr– June & Sept–Oct 8.30am–5pm; July &

Vienna

Aug 8.30am–6pm; Nov–Mar
8.30am–4.30pm.
Admission charge. U4: Schönbrunn; U4,
tram 10, 58 & 60: Hietzing.

Sezessionhaus (Secession Building)

A courageous group of Viennese artists, inspired by the *Jugendstil*/Art Nouveau movement, set out to change the world in 1897. They broke their ties with Vienna's art establishment and the eclectic styles of the Ringstrasse to form a new art association called 'Secession'. The following year, architect Joseph Maria Olbrich erected an Art Nouveau temple for the movement – the Sezessionhaus – using modern materials and building techniques such as glass and steel. The only permanent exhibit, in the basement, is a 34m (112ft) *Beethoven Frieze* by Secession leader Gustav Klimt: a visual interpretation of the final chorale of Beethoven's 9th Symphony.
Friedrichstrasse 12. Tel: 587 53 07. www.secession.at. Open: Tue–Sun 10am–6pm, Thur 10am–8pm. Closed: Mon. Bus: Karlsplatz/Oper.

Stephansdom

Steffl, as the Viennese call their cathedral, is the symbol of Vienna and Austria's most famous Gothic building. The current structure is actually the third church to be erected on this site, beginning with a simple Romanesque basilica built in 1147. Part of a second Romanesque church now forms the west façade. Among the cathedral's wealth of art treasures are the tombs of Emperor Frederick III and Prince Eugene of Savoy (1754), the remarkable pulpit by Anton Pilgram, and the Wiener Neustädter Altar (Wiener Neustadt Altarpiece), a Gothic winged altar from 1447. The cathedral suffered damage during the Turkish siege of 1683 and again in the closing days of World War II, when fire from streetfighting leapt to the rooftop. The cathedral was reopened in 1948, and the roof was repaired and decorated with ceramic tiles donated by Viennese citizens in 1950. Mozart was married here in 1782, and his funeral was held here in December 1791. You can ascend both towers.

Stephansdom, with its ornate Gothic façade

The North Tower, reached by lift, holds the Pummerin bell, one of the largest bells in the world. It is only rung once a year – on New Year's Eve. The tower has a fine view of Vienna and the Vienna Woods. The view from the South Tower is even better, but you have to climb 343 spiral steps to reach it.

Stephansplatz. Tel: 515 52 35 26. www.stephanskirche.at. U1 & U3: Stephansplatz.
Cathedral. Open: to visitors Mon–Sat 6am–10pm, Sun 7am–10pm. During services, you are not allowed to enter the main nave unless you are attending worship.
North Tower. Open: 8.30am–5.30pm. South Tower. Open: 9am–5.30pm. Catacomb tours every 30 mins Mon–Sat 10–11.30am & 1.30–4.30pm, Sun 1.30–4.30pm. Admission charge for towers, catacombs and treasury.

Getting away: Vienna Woods

Vienna is located on the slopes of the Vienna Woods. The favourite mountains are the Leopoldsberg and Kahlenberg, where you can enjoy the magnificent view of the city. The Vienna Woods are crisscrossed by a network of marked walking and hiking paths, easily reached with Vienna's public transportation. These *Stadtwanderwege* (city paths) cover areas ranging from the vineyard-studded Kahlenberg hill in the city's northwest to the forested Zugberg in the south. There are 13 hikes, with walking times from 2½ hours to

5 hours, and distances of 4–6km (2½–4 miles). They feature their own, little-known sights, including ancient churches, castles and a historical observatory. Remarkably, you can also go around or traverse the Austrian capital – north to south and east to west – staying almost entirely in parks or woods.

Unusually for a metropolis, Vienna has a wine region within the city limits. Vineyards that harvest their wine in or around Vienna may call themselves *Heuriger* (this means both 'this year's wine' and the 'wine tavern' where it is served). It is prohibited to add other grapes or wine to the local vintage if you want to sell it. On spring and summer evenings in particular, the Viennese flock to the wine gardens to quaff the *Heuriger* wines, but the wine taverns, also called *Buschenschanken*, are open all year round. 'New' wine becomes old wine – called *Alter* – after St Martin's Day (11 November). Several *Heurigen* can be found north of the city in Stammersdorf – there are some in the main street (*tram 31, followed by a short walk*).

VIENNA HIKING

For information and maps for various walks in Vienna visit:
www.wien.gv.at/wald/wandern/wege.htm
www.wien.gv.at/english/leisure/hiking/wege.htm
www.wienguide.at/pages/englisch/englisch.html
Also visit *www.vienna.info* for more information.

Wachau

The Wachau is a 35km (22-mile) stretch of the Danube Valley between Melk and Krems – an enchanted river landscape packed with cliffs, castles, vines, Baroque spires, riverside villages and holy places. Its compact size makes it very easy to get around by car, train, boat and bike, or even on foot. It's also quite easy to combine transportation methods between riverside towns and villages that offer an ensemble of architecture from Gothic to Renaissance, Baroque and Biedermeier.

The terraced vineyards and orchards of the Wachau are particularly beautiful in spring when the peaches and apricots bloom, or in autumn when the vine leaves turn golden. The valley has been fertile ground for piety as well as wine since monks first planted wine grapes here in the 8th century. The monumental abbey of Melk,

high on a cliff above the Danube, bears witness to the Wachau's cultural and spiritual importance. It has been an active Benedictine monastery for nearly 1,000 years.

No other wine region in Austria possesses such a density of medieval towns and villages, and there are dozens of wine festivals between May and

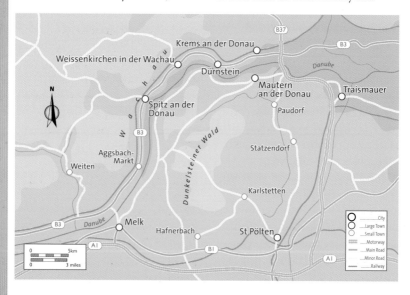

The ruined castle looms over Dürnstein

November. The riverside train tracks and bike paths follow the Danube's loops through vineyards and forests, skirting ancient city walls and passing beneath feudal towers. The distances are short but there is much to see. A tour of the region's cellars could take many days and it is hard to say which is most impressive – the architecture, local hospitality, or wines by the glass.

Dürnstein

Competing with Melk for the title of Wachau's 'most beautiful' (and touristy) town, Dürnstein is still folded inside its medieval walls and, seemingly, in a time warp. The ancient ramparts straggle up to the ruined castle where Richard the Lionheart was imprisoned in the 12th century by the Austrian Emperor Leopold V. Legend has it that he was angry at Richard for cheating him out of his fair share of crusader spoils. Some of the vast sum that the English paid in ransom was used to build the city walls that once encircled Vienna. The town of Dürnstein has many richly decorated 15th-century houses. The Baroque parish church, Maria Himmelfahrt, with its iconic pastel-blue spire, was once part of the Augustinian monastery.

Krems an der Donau

Krems, which marks one end of the Wachau, consists of three small towns – Krems, Und and Stein. This three-in-one town is also perhaps the best base for wine tourism because it is at the convergence of three wine regions: the Wachau itself and the Krems and Kamp valleys. Krems and Stein were once extremely rich thanks to taxes from river traffic – those who could not pay had their cargo confiscated. In the early 11th century, the first mint of Austria was established in Krems. The Steiner Tor (town gate) was constructed in the 15th century as part of the town's fortifications. Krems has two churches of interest as well as a museum housed in a former Dominican monastery. It contains religious art from the Middle Ages and historic odds and ends going back to the days of Roman settlement. There is also a replica of fertility goddess 'Fanny' vom Galgenberg said to be 32,000 years old. A fascinating exhibit covers the history of viticulture in the Wachau since the days of the Roman empire.

Melk

The Benedictine monastery at Melk has been an important spiritual and cultural centre for almost 1,000 years. The monastery began as a Roman fortress and became the seat of the Babenberg court from 976 to 1089 until Leopold II gave the fortress to the Benedictine order. Monks still live and worship here.

The monastery was rebuilt several times, and transformed in 1702 by Jakob Prantauer into the Baroque masterpiece you see today. Visitors can explore several rooms of exhibits that describe the history of the monastery, before stepping out onto the monastery's balcony overlooking the Danube and the village of Melk below.

For a Benedictine monastery, the library is the most important part – after the Basilica of course. The 100,000-volume library here is spread across twelve rooms on three floors. The Baroque artists, masters of illusion,

View across Krems to the Danube

painted the flat library ceilings to appear domed. A final stop in the monastery's lavishly gilded Baroque church completes the tour.

The town of Melk also merits a visit.

Spitz an der Donau

Spitz is an historic town, remarkably well preserved and surrounded by leafy vineyards, one of which is known as the Tausendeimerberg (Thousand Buckets Mountain). It is well worth the steep hike up to the ruins of the once massive 13th-century Burg Hinterhaus. St Mauritius, the late-Gothic parish church at the far end of the village, contains numerous religious treasures including carved wooden figures of Jesus and his 12 Apostles in niches in a Gothic gallery.

The Benedictine monastery, Melk

Cycle: Melk or Spitz to Krems

This section of the Donau-Radwanderweg (Danube bike path) is one of the most popular in Europe. It winds along vineyards, through small towns and below medieval castles. You can rent a bike in Vienna (www. pedalpower.at) and take it with you, or in Melk (Hotel zur Post. www.post-melk.at) or Spitz (Thomas Bernhardt. Tel: 02713 22 22. www.wachau-touristik.at); call ahead to reserve. The entire area blooms during the apricot blossom in spring. Otherwise, go in June or September.

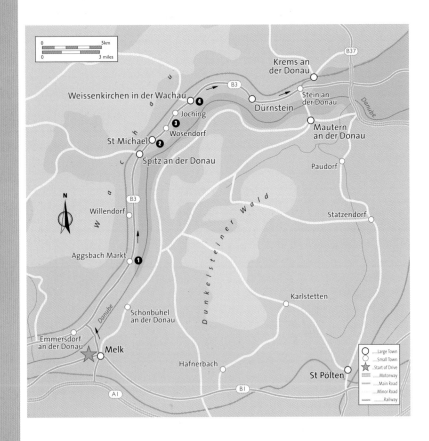

The cycle ride takes 3 hours from Melk to Krems or 90 minutes from Spitz to Krems.

Starting from Melk, cross over to the north side (Emmersdorf) then head downstream. The path runs north along the Danube to Aggsbach Markt.

1 Aggsbach Markt

Aggsbach was first officially mentioned in AD 830, but it is best known for something that happened 24,000 years ago in nearby Willendorf. Some mammoth hunters left behind a fertility statue now known as the 'Venus of Willendorf'. There is a small museum with a copy of the statue and details of its discovery (the original is now in Vienna's Natural History Museum). *The bike path continues running along the Danube to Spitz an der Donau (see p51) then to St Michael.*

2 St Michael

The tiny village of St Michael (36 inhabitants!) possesses a remarkable church that provides a Gothic contrast to the Baroque wonders of Melk, across the river. It was the original parish church of the Wachau region, built in the 10th century. Most of what you see today dates from 1500. The meaning of the seven stone creatures on the ridge of the church's roof remains an unsolved riddle. Behind the church are a charnel house and a round Gothic tower. *Carry on along the path to Wösendorf and Joching.*

3 Wösendorf and Joching

These two nearly adjacent villages produce the legendary Riesling wine grape, which is said to have been planted here for the first time in 1232. Rejoin the path and ride to Weissenkirchen in der Wachau.

4 Weissenkirchen in der Wachau

Weissenkirchen is the centre of the Wachau, and it produces some of its best wines. Its Gothic fortified church successfully held off the besieging Turks in 1531. The town has a medley of historic buildings including a number of Renaissance mansions. The Teisenhoferhof (*Weissenkirchen 177*) is a fortified estate from the same era, containing a small museum and cultural centre. There is a display by 19th- and 20th-century Wachau painters. *Follow the bike path as it loops around the Danube through Dürnstein, Stein an der Donau and, finally, Krems (see p50).*

Vineyards surround Weissenkirchen

Austrian wines

Austria's best wines are on the wine lists of many of the world's top restaurants. They are especially known for the way they complement food, for example with foie gras and fish as well as Asian cuisines.

Wachau

There are about ten different wine regions in Austria of note and all are in Eastern Austria, wrapped around the capital, Vienna. The best-known region is the Wachau, west of Vienna, where the sloping vineyards overlook the Danube. The finest wines of the Wachau come from the steep, terraced slopes that make up a good proportion of the vines in the area. This region has its own specific classifications: *Steinfeder* (light and fresh), *Federspiel* (elegant, medium-bodied) and *Smaragd* (full-bodied, powerful).

Equally good wines are made in Kremstal and then the Kamptal, two valleys that feed into the Wachau on the north side. Wine connoisseurs, after studiously sniffing and parsing a glass of Wachau's best, will detect, beyond the perfume of peaches and apricots, a multitude of exotic fruit and mineral notes. Although Riesling

Vines at Weissenkirchen in der Wachau

The vineyards of Burgenland

only represents 15 per cent of the vine area of the Wachau, it is considered by most top Wachau winemakers to be the finest wine they can produce. Riesling suits the soils that dominate the area, but Grüner Veltliner is the quintessentially Austrian grape, and it often produces a light, easy to drink wine. Yet in the hands of the top growers of the Wachau, Grüner Veltliner acquires the depth and fruit to age gracefully.

Burgenland

South of Vienna in Burgenland province, the eastern shore around the Neusiedl Lake – the only central European steppe lake – is almost entirely planted with vines. The shallow lake offers ideal conditions for the development of botrytis (noble rot) on grapes, a precondition for creating its world-class, naturally sweet wines: Beerenauslese, Trockenbeerenauslese, the rare Ausbruch and even rarer Schilfwein (reed wine – a sweet wine made from grapes dried on beds of reeds).

The majority of Austria's best red wines are produced to the south of Neusiedl Lake in Middle Burgenland, some of them from vines up to 80 years old.

A group of top red wine producers in Middle Burgenland has created a rich, barrel-aged Austrian blend called *Pannobile*.

Burgenland

Burgenland (Land of Castles) stretches to the southeast of Vienna towards Hungary, an area of vineyards and orchards, spas, small towns and, yes, castles. Austria's summers are at their hottest in the northern part of Burgenland around Neusiedl, the largest steppe lake in Central Europe. While it is relatively unknown to foreign tourists, the Viennese come here to relax on weekends and in summer.

The atmosphere in this border region is a reminder of the days when Austria was a dual Austro-Hungarian monarchy. The people of the region voted to join Austria after World War I, but the residents of its ancient capital (Sopron) opted to remain in neighbouring Hungary. Burgenland itself feels like Hungary in places, with its flat steppe, gypsy music and goulash. The Austrian capital of Burgenland is Eisenstadt, a small provincial city. It was here that court composer Joseph Haydn created the

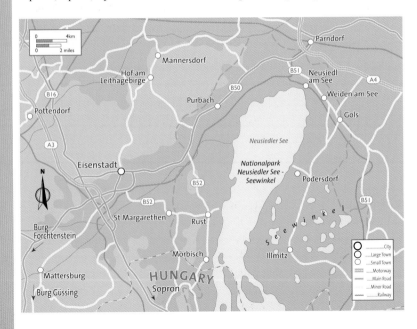

Schloss Esterházy in Eisenstadt

string quartet and the early classical symphony.

Burgenland's largest natural feature is shallow Neusiedler See (Neusiedl Lake) – the 'Sea of the Viennese'. Despite its vast size, this mysterious body of water has an odd habit of disappearing completely, most recently in the beginning of the 20th century. For the migration of birds, this wetland is immensely important. Waders are among the typical summer guests, and in autumn thousands of wild geese offer a memorable spectacle as they descend on the shores. Lake Neusiedl National Park is not only famous for its many species of birds and plants, some of which are rare, but also for wine. Due to the evaporation of its waters, the high humidity in the northern Burgenland is perfect for the production of sweet, Sauternes-style white wines. This mostly flat province is also blessed with low-lying hills rich in soils that nurture indigenous red grape varieties.

In 2004, with Hungary joining the EU and the opening of its borders with Austria, Burgenland regained its historical character as a bridge between the two countries.

Burg Forchtenstein

In this land of castles, the fortress of Forchtenstein has no equal. Visible from afar on its high dolomite crag, it served as the treasury and arsenal of the earls of Esterházy, one of the wealthiest dynasties in European history (it still belongs to the family). The castle was actually built by the counts of Mattersdorf but sold, in 1445, to the Habsburgs, who gave it to the Esterházys. They expanded it constantly between 1635 and 1652, making it impregnable against the invading Turks, and filling it with the largest arsenal in central Europe. Today, it ranks as one of Europe's most impressive collections. The star attraction is the restored picture gallery with an astonishing 230 life-size family portraits, including one of the count who inspired the Dracula legend.

Melinda Esterházy-Platz 1. Tel: 02626 81 21 2. www.burg-forchtenstein.at. Open: 10am–6pm. Closed: Nov–Mar. Admission charge.

Burg Güssing

One of Burgenland's most impressive sights, this castle looks down on the surrounding countryside from the mouth of an extinct volcano. Starting in 1524, it was the ancestral seat of the counts of Batthyánys, a family destined to play a prominent part in Hungarian history (the Habsburg Emperor had Lajos Batthyány, the first prime minister of Hungary, executed by firing squad in 1849). Many generations of Batthyánys are on display in the picture gallery of the Rittersaal (Knights' Hall). Architecturally, its towers, parapets and gabled buildings date mostly from the 16th and 17th centuries when the Turkish threat was at its height, and up to 3,000 people called it home. So-called Batthyány porcelain is also on display, snow-white with a simple pattern of gilded leaves and tiny fan-shaped tiny flowers.

Batthyánystr 10. Tel: 03322 43 40 0. www.burgguessing.info.

The frescoed hall used by Haydn at Schloss Esterházy

The imposing Burg Forchtenstein

Open: Easter–end Oct 10am–5pm.
Closed: Mon. Admission charge.

Eisenstadt

The capital of Burgenland province since its partition after World War I, Eisenstadt dates back to at least 1118. It experienced a golden age in the 17th century when it became the residence of the Esterházys and, for 31 years, their court composer Joseph Haydn. You can visit Schloss Esterházy by guided tour where Haydn debuted many of his works in a frescoed hall with extraordinary acoustics. Haydn's residence, Haydn Haus, is a small museum, and he is buried in the Bergkirche, the Baroque hilltop church just southwest of town. A Haydn festival (*www.haydnfestival.at*), which takes place in September, features

performances in both the palace and the church.

Other points of interest are the town itself with a Baroque Rathaus (Town Hall) decorated with folk paintings of the 'seven virtues', and the Austrian Jewish Museum – it occupies the one-time mansion of Rabbi Samson Wertheimer (1658–1713), chief administrator of financial affairs for three Habsburg emperors.

Schloss Esterházy. Tel: 02682 67 39 0.
www.schloss-esterhazy.at. Open: mid-Mar–mid-Nov daily 8.30am–6pm; mid-Nov–mid-Mar Mon–Thur 9am–5pm, Fri 9am–3pm. Closed: Sat & Sun.
Admission charge.

Haydn House. 21 Joseph Haydngasse.
Tel: 02682 67 39 0. Open: mid-Mar–mid-Nov daily 9am–5pm.
Closed: Winter. Admission charge.

Typical Baroque architectural decoration in Rust

Austrian Jewish Museum,
6 Unterbergstrasse.
Tel: 02682 65 14 5. www.ojm.at.
Open: May–Oct 10am–5pm.
Closed: Mon. Admission charge.

Mörbisch

Surrounded by vineyards lies Mörbisch, a charming little town of long, narrow lanes and whitewashed, arcaded houses in traditional Burgenland style. A long (almost 2km/1¼ miles) causeway leads to an island bathing beach with excellent facilities for water sports, including surfing and sailing. A floating stage is the setting for performances of operettas (Mörbischer Seefestspiele) in August.

Neusiedler See (Neusiedl Lake)

The Neusiedl steppe lake straddling the border between Austria and Hungary extends to 315sq km (121 sq miles) of which 240sq km (93 sq miles) are in Austria. Never more than 1.8m (6ft) deep, it is ringed by wetlands that provide a breeding ground for nearly 300 species of birds. Hikers and bikers use the causeways and trails that wind through the reeds and grasslands for miles, and the beaches draw crowds in summer. In winter, there is ice-yachting and skate-sailing. Neusiedl National Park is the largest bird sanctuary in central Europe, with a surface area of 14,000ha (34,594 acres), 6,000ha (14,826 acres) of them on Hungarian territory. It is a popular recreation area as well as a wildlife zone, and you can hire boats and sailboards at points all around the lake. The water quality varies greatly depending on the amount of salt and mud emanating from sediments in the ground. During the summer months, there is a risk of dry reed fires that can spread quickly because of the wind.

Rust

The town has many subtle architectural details from its long history – ornamented doorways, Baroque oriels, and inner courtyards that have a secretive feeling. The fortified fishermen's church has some noteworthy medieval frescoes and a Gothic altar. Storks nest each spring on the rooftops of the Old Town centre, and stay until their chicks are ready to fly south in September.

Rust's (pronounced Roosht) claim to fame is a centuries-old tradition of producing sweet wines such as Ruster Ausbruch, which is similar to Tokay. Rust is the location of the Austrian Wine Academy, which was the first teaching institution of its kind in a German-speaking country.

Neusiedl Lake, central Europe's most important wetland, is disappearing. Two studies conducted by a group of experts at the University of Vienna concluded that, under the impact of global warming, Neusiedl Lake will dry up at some point between 2010 and 2050. There is a plan to save it with infusions of water from the Danube River, but the project poses a potential risk to the lake's fragile ecosystem.

Drive: Burgenland

Neusiedl Lake is a great place for nature- and wine-lovers. A tour of the area could include birdwatching, swimming (in summer) or skating (in winter), and tasting wine in some of Austria's most heralded vineyards. There are wine taverns all around the lake, many with excellent food.

Allow at least a day for this drive.

From Eisenstadt, take the B52 east through a stretch of hills and vineyards to St Margarethen.

1 St Margarethen

This 1st-century Roman quarry (*www.roemersteinbruch.at*), which also provided the stone for the Votivkirche in Vienna, is now a workshop for artists of different nationalities. A passion play has been presented here each summer for over 70 years.
Carry on to Rust (see p61), then drive north to the fork with the B52, looping around the lake on the B50 and B51 to Neusiedl am See.

2 Neusiedl am See

Although it's a bit of a walk through the reeds to the water, this town specialises in all sorts of water sports including sailing and surfing. In the case of inclement weather, there is a state-of-the art indoor swimming pool and the Pannonisches Heimatmuseum (*Kalvarienbergstrasse 40*), dedicated to folk arts and customs. Inside the Gothic parish church is a curious Baroque pulpit in the shape of a ship.

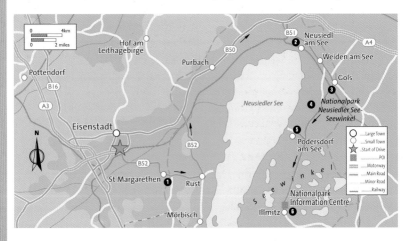

Drive southeast around the lake (still on the B51), passing Weiden am See, and follow signs for Gols.

3 Gols

Wine has been the primary source of livelihood for over 2,000 years in Gols on the sun-drenched northeastern side of the lake. The town is home to the founding members of the Pannobile Association, devoted to promoting earthy reds made from Austrian varieties, Zweigelt and Blaufrankisch.
Take Scheunegasse to get back on the B51 going south to Nationalpark Neusiedler See-Seewinkel.

4 Nationalpark Neusiedler See-Seewinkel

The Zitzmannsdorf meadowland is a birdwatcher's paradise. There are also many rare plants here. It is part of the Seewinkel, an area of protected wetlands interspersed with vines, which extends around much of the eastern shore. Spring is the best time to visit.
Continue just 3km (2 miles) to Podersdorf.

5 Podersdorf am See

If Neusiedl Lake is a 'Viennese Sea', Podersdorf is the Viennese 'seaside' since it is the only town with direct access to the lake shore. The town is also a point of departure for bike tours and boat cruises that stop at Illmitz and, on the western shore, Mörbisch and Rust. The boats allow bikes so you can combine the two. Podersdorf also serves as a gateway to the Seewinkel bird sanctuary and national park.
Take Obere Haupstrasse and drive 11km (7 miles) further south to Illmitz.

6 Illmitz

This is the lowest point in Austria, surrounded by 20 small marsh lakes in addition to Neusiedl. The lakes give off humidity following a hot summer, which is good for making nectar-like dessert wines. Locally grown walnuts, a Burgenland staple, are used in everything from bread to pasta sauce. Birdwatchers should head straight to the north side of town and the Nationalpark Information Centre (*Hauswiese. Tel: 02175 34 42 0. www.nationalpark-neusiedlersee-seewinkel.at. Open: 8am–5pm, shorter hours in winter*).

Wetlands at Seewinkel

Salzburg

The legendary traveller Alexander von Humboldt called Salzburg one of the seven most beautiful places on earth. Although it was a Celtic and Roman settlement, its glory days began in the Middle Ages when it became both a bishopric and fabulously rich from its trade in salt. At its height, Salzburg was the capital of a powerful clerical state that included parts of the Tyrol and Italy.

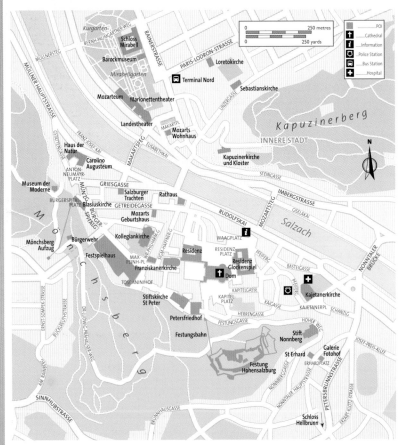

Salzburg's cathedral

The ruling prince-archbishops, inspired by Italian models, built a 'German Rome' at the foot of the Alps, a quintessentially Baroque city of fountains, domes and church spires crowned by an impregnable fortress, the Festung Hohensalzburg. The clerical realm only became part of Austria in 1816. 'Happiness lives here, nothing evil enters', says a Roman inscription dug up in the 19th century in a city square. No tourist brochure could put it better. Today, 'all Salzburg is a stage' that honours (and crassly exploits) its native son, Mozart. In summer, it is the setting for one of Europe's elite music festivals, the Salzburger Festspiele.

Dom (Cathedral)

The cathedral is the most impressive early Baroque church north of the Alps. St Virgil built the first church on the spot in 774, but it, and many successors, burned down. The crypt has previous churches' floor plans inlaid in the pavement beneath the central rotunda. Santino Solari designed the present cathedral, which was begun in 1614 under prince archbishop Markus

Sittikus and consecrated in 1628 by archbishop Paris Lodron. The magnificent dome was largely destroyed in one of 19 attacks by Allied bombers in World War II but was later painstakingly restored. The Dommuseum (Cathedral Museum and Treasury, entrance in the vestibule) holds holy treasures collected by the archbishops from the Middle Ages to the 19th century, and the secular Kunst und Wunderkammer (Art and Rarities Collection) is from the 17th and 18th centuries.

Dom. Domplatz. Tel: 0662 8047 7950.
Open: summer daily 6.30am–7pm,
winter daily 6.30am–5pm.
Free admission.
Dommuseum. Domplatz. Tel: 0662 8047 1870. Open: May–end Oct & Dec–early Jan Mon–Sat 10am–5pm,
Sun & hols 11am–6pm.
Admission charge.

Festung Hohensalzburg

The largest fully preserved fortress in central Europe (*c.*1077) was built to protect Salzburg's ruling prince-archbishops from their enemies and, as need be, from their own parishioners. The prince-archbishop Leonhard von Keutschach greatly expanded the fortress in 1500 (his symbol was the turnip – you will see turnips carved all over the castle). The fortress grounds are open to the public and you are free to wander around its courtyards, narrow lanes and ramparts. The fortress was a city unto itself with its own bakery, blacksmith, armoury, granary and stables. A tour of the castle inside begins with a look at seven historic models, from crude beginnings in wood to the mighty stone edifice of today. It continues on to the torture chambers, the prison tower, the staterooms and the Golden Chamber

The view from the Festung Hohensalzburg

(with a pillar damaged by a cannonball during the Peasants' Revolt of 1525). There are two small museums that underwhelm: the Rainer Regimental Museum follows one regiment through centuries of military history, and a small Castle Museum contains historic odds and ends – the most interesting relate to the all-powerful prince-archbishop Wolf Dietrich von Raitenau, whose career ended in the castle dungeon. *Mönchsberg 34. Tel: 0662 8424 3011. www.salzburg-burgen.at. Open: July–Sept 8am–9pm; Nov–Mar 9am–5pm; Apr–June & Oct 9am–6pm. Admission charge.*

Franziskanerkirche

Architecturally speaking, the Franciscan Church is an interminable lesson in art history in which many styles have been given equal time. Surprisingly, the end effect is one of deep harmony. The first church was founded during the 8th century and destroyed by fire in 1167. The dark Romanesque nave (built in 1223) gives way to a brilliantly illuminated late Gothic choir (1408–60); the Baroque high altar by Fischer von Erlach (1709) was created to hold a far older Madonna.

Getreidegasse

The elaborately ornamented signs (one of the largest belongs to McDonald's), finely carved portals and arcaded courtyards add a decorative touch to the main business of shopping in this street. Wolfgang

The many architectural styles of the Franziskanerkirche

Amadeus, one of seven children, was born to Leopold and Anna Mozart in 1756 in **Mozarts Geburtshaus**, a third-floor apartment at No 9. The family lived there until 1773, when they moved across the river. Mozart's birthplace is now a museum, where visitors can see Mozart family portraits, his childhood violin and clavichord and the rooms where he lived and wrote music – Mozart composed his first piece when he was just four years old.
Mozarts Geburtshaus. Getreidegasse 9. Tel: 0662 84 43 13. www.mozarteum.at. Open: Sept–June 9am–6pm; July & Aug 9am–7pm. Admission charge.

Mozarts Wohnhaus

World War II bombing raids all but destroyed the house that was the second home of Mozart (his family moved there in 1773, when he was 17), and this is largely a reconstruction. The exhibits do not justify the price of admission but an audio phone recording and film provide a moving account of Mozart's family life, although you might want to turn down the volume during the gushy coda of Salzburg PR.

Makartplatz 8. Tel: 0662 8742 2740. www.mozarteum.at. Open: 9am–6pm; July & Aug until 7pm. Admission charge.

Museum der Moderne (Modern Art Museum), Mönchsberg

The museum merits a visit for the view alone, particularly from the rooftop terrace, but there's a lot more to see.

Petersfriedhof, carved out of the cliffs

The collection ranges from turn-of-the-last-century artists such as Klimt, Kokoschka and Alfred Kubin, through Austrian expressionists like Herbert Boeckl, Eduard Bäumer and Hans Fronius, to contemporary works such as the 'embryo worlds' of Bruno Gironcoli, Heimo Zobernig video installations, and photography by Cindy Sherman.

Mönchsberg 32. Take the lift from Anton-Neumayr-Platz. Tel: 0662 8422 20403. www.museumdermoderne.at. Open: Tue & Thur–Sun 10am–6pm, Wed 10am–9pm. Closed: Mon. Admission charge.

Statues of Greek mythological figures dot the Mirabell Gardens

Petersfriedhof

There is no better place to contemplate the particularly Austrian fascination with death than at St Peter's, one of the oldest and most beautiful cemeteries in the world. Its origins go back at least as far as the days of the Roman settlement, Juvavum. 'Sealed in dreams' is how Salzburg poet Georg Trakl described it. Early Christians carved out the first tombs and cells – the **Katakomben** – in the cliff of Mönchsberg (*Open: May–Sept Tue–Sun 10.30am–5pm. Shorter hours in winter. Admission charge*). The elegant arcades that now line the cliff were built over 1,000 years later. Many generations of Salzburgers lie buried beneath them, including Santino Solari (the cathedral architect), Nannerl Mozart (Mozart's sister) and Michael Haydn (younger brother of Joseph Haydn). In the middle of the graveyard, the Gothic Margarethenkapelle is all but draped in delicately carved tombstones.

Next to Stiftskirche St Peter. Tel: 0662 8445 7689. www.stift-stpeter.at (German only). Open: Apr–Sept 6.30am–7pm; shorter hours in winter. Free admission.

Residenz

Prince-archbishop Wolf Dietrich von Raitenau had this palace built in 1595 on the site of an earlier one. Its modest exterior hides magnificent chambers and vast swathes of pomp – ornate chairs beneath frescoed ceilings, Gobelin tapestries, and curiosities like a

Schloss Mirabell and Gardens

brass balustrade that has been 'tuned'. The northwest wing was added in the 18th century. The **Residenz Gallery** (Art Gallery) has an interesting but not unmissable collection of European paintings from the 16th to the 19th centuries, with a couple of Dutch and Flemish masters (Rembrandt, Rubens), and Italian, French and Austrian works from the 19th century (Amerling, Ender, Waldmüller). Paintings to look out for are: Rembrandt's *Rembrandts Mutter*, Paulus Potter's *Viehaustrieb*;

Gaspard Dughet's *Heroische Landschaft mit Figuren*; Ferdinand Georg Waldmüller's *Kinder im Fenster*, and Hans Makart's *Gesellschaftsszene*. *Residenzplatz 1. Tel: 0662 8404 510. www.residenzgalerie.at. Open: 10am–5pm. Residenz Gallery. Closed: Oct–Mar. Admission charge.*

Schloss Mirabell (Mirabell Palace) and Gardens

The prince-archbishops who ruled Salzburg, for all their power, obviously could not marry. Most of them kept several *Schlafweiber* (bed wenches) who discreetly used the servants' back door. Wolf Dietrich von Raitenau broke with this 'tradition' by loving a woman openly and faithfully – Salome Alt, a merchant's daughter – and acknowledging the 16 children he had with her. He went so far as to build a palace and gardens for her in 1606, the Altenau, later renamed Mirabell. The palace was substantially remodelled in 1721–7, and again in 1818 after a disastrous town fire. The symmetrical Mirabell Gardens are adorned with figures from Greek mythology and huge marble vases. The Zwerglgarten, an 18th-century collection of grotesque garden gnomes, provides comic relief.

Somewhat more highbrow, the **Salzburg Barockmuseum** has a small but rewarding 17th- to 18th-century collection of European art (*Tel: 0662 87 74 32. www.barockmuseum.at. Open: Tue–Sun 10am–5pm. Admission charge*). The palace itself, now the Town Hall, is most interesting for its monumental staircase. The figures – larger-than-life Roman goddesses and proud heroes with bulging thighs – are by Georg Raphael Donner. He also carved a dozen chubby *putti* for the staircase banisters, who raise their fingers and seem to smile at the visitor. The Marble Hall, on the second floor, is used for weddings and concerts.

Mirabellplatz. Tel: 0662 8072 2334. Open: Mon, Wed & Sun 8am–4pm, Tue & Fri 1–4pm, Sat 8am–1pm. Free admission.

Stiftskirche St Peter

This Benedictine abbey church belongs to one of the oldest monasteries north of the Alps (*c.*800). Two major Baroque facelifts and the addition of a dome fail to completely obscure the massiveness and geometry of the original Romanesque, triple-aisled basilica. Look out for the Roman tombstones used as building blocks in the walls of the main portal. Inside, there are no

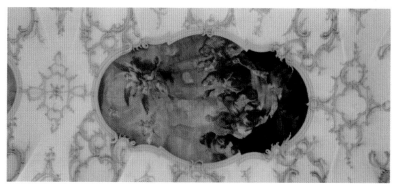

One of the nave ceiling frescoes in Stiftskirche St Peter

fewer than 15 side altars. One of them, in the south aisle, is said to contain the tomb of St Rupert. The decoration of the central nave with so many works on canvas is something of an anomaly. The canvases tell the life stories of Saints Rupert and Benedict. The frescoes on the ceiling of the nave depict scenes from the life of St Peter. The grille between the porch and nave is a famous example of wrought-ironwork.

Erzabtei St Peter. Tel: 0662 84 45 76. Open: daily 8am–noon & 4.30–6.30pm. Free admission.

Schloss Hellbrunn and Gardens

This early Baroque pleasure palace was built by Santino Solari (1612–15) for the hedonistic prince-archbishop and ladies' man Markus Sittikus, who loved all things Italian and, seemingly, all things pagan. His extensive Baroque gardens are filled with mechanical and natural wonders – grottoes devoted to Neptune and Orpheus, marble Roman goddesses and naughty stone satyrs, rare plants, and the famous trick fountains. Despite being a man of God, Sittikus was full of mischief. He built gardens that let him play practical jokes on his friends and guests. His fountains are a most unusual form of tourist trap – they spray water on unsuspecting visitors. It is also water that moves the figures in the Mechanical Theatre. For 200 years, every important visitor to Salzburg's court was brought here, including, one imagines, Mozart. The trick water gardens are the most

renowned part of the palace. There are a dozen different *Wasserspiele* (water jokes). Don't accept the offer to sit at the table in the outdoor amphitheatre. Water spurting up from the seats was meant to soak the summer finery of the prince-archbishop's guests. If they leapt up, other fountains squirted them from the floor. It's the kind of joke Mozart would have loved. Hellbrunn's other water-driven marvel is the Mechanical Theatre in which 200 automated wooden figures move to music from a hydraulically operated organ.

Schloss Hellbrunn Fürstenweg 37. Located 5km (3 miles) south of the Altstadt (Old Town). Tel: 0662 82 03 7 20. www.hellbrunn.at. Open: Mar, Apr & Oct 9am–4.30pm; May, June & Sept 9am–5.30pm; July & Aug 9am–10pm (trick fountains only from 6pm). Admission charge.

THE SOUND OF MUSIC

Most Austrians have never seen *The Sound of Music*, which was filmed in and around Salzburg. By contrast, an estimated 90 per cent of the Americans who visit the city go on a 'Sound of Music' tour. For the record, a musically gifted von Trapp family fled Austria in 1938. But the Nazis were not in hot pursuit; nor did nuns sabotage the von Trapps' car. The von Trapps never profited from the film starring Julie Andrews and Christopher Plummer, the most successful musical in the history of Hollywood. They had already sold the rights to their story (for $10,000) to a German company. The descendants of the von Trapp family run a hotel in Vermont.

Beware of the fountains at Schloss Hellbrunn

Walk: Squares of Salzburg

The Altstadt (Old Town) of Salzburg is mostly a pedestrian zone linking Salzburg's Baroque squares. Prince-archbishop Wolf Dietrich von Raitenau was determined to make Salzburg look like Rome, and had a couple of hundred medieval houses knocked down to make room for the squares.

Allow half a day.

1 Domplatz

The Domplatz (Cathedral Square) is where the *Jedermann* is staged during the Salzburg Festival, with the façade of the cathedral as a backdrop. In 1756,

Mozart was baptised in the huge bronze baptismal font that is to the left as you enter the cathedral.

Go right (south), passing the Italianate arches of the cathedral, to Kapitelplatz.

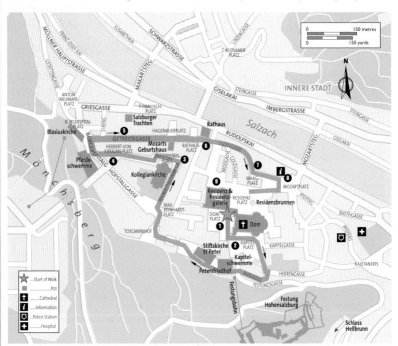

2 Kapitelplatz

The elegant fountain in the corner, Kapitelschwemme, was used to water the horses of the prince-archbishops. The funicular that ascends to the fortress of Hohensalzburg (more than a century old but still well oiled) is across the square in the Festungsgasse.

Follow Festungsgasse around a bend and enter Petersfriedhof (St Peter's Cemetery). Continue downhill through the cemetery to Stiftskirche St Peter. The next square is Max Reinhardt Platz. Walk downhill (north) to the right of the church and into Universitätsplatz.

3 Universitätsplatz

The Kollegiankirche (1696–1707), by Fischer von Erlach, dominates the square. Architecturally, the church is a masterpiece that influenced many other Baroque churches in Austria,

Domplatz in Salzburg's Old Town

southern Germany and Prague, with its geometric forms and undulating, convex façade that rises dynamically to its towers. The farmers' market (*Closed: Sun*) is an excellent place for a quick lunch.

Continue past the fountain to the end of the square. Cross the big road to Herbert-von-Karajan-Platz.

4 Herbert-von-Karajan-Platz

The giant horse troughs, also by von Erlach, are one of Salzburg's most famous sites. They sum up the Baroque, Austrian obsession with all things equestrian.

Cross the road again and take two right turns into Getreidegasse.

5 Getreidegasse

Walking down this narrow street will remind you that the medieval city, wedged between Mönchsberg and the Salzach River, could only expand in one direction. Outwardly, it has changed little since Mozart was born at No 9 (*see p67*).

Continue east along Getreidegasse to the Rathausplatz.

6 Rathausplatz

The modest Rathaus (Town Hall) pales in comparison to the grand monuments of the prince-archbishops. Cross the square and continue in the same direction down into Judengasse, once the heart of a Jewish community first mentioned in 1284. The synagogue was at No 15 until 1415 (now the Gasthof

Höllbräu). Large numbers of Jews were executed in 1349 and 1404. In 1498, prince-archbishop Leonhard von Keutschach banned Jews from his realm 'forever and eternally'.

Follow Judengasse around a bend to Waagplatz.

7 Waagplatz

This square was the commercial nexus of medieval Salzburg, where goods were weighed for taxation and grain hoarded in the attic. No 4 has a Roman cellar used for art exhibitions.

Continue to the end of the square to Mozartplatz.

8 Mozartplatz

Were he alive to see it, Mozart would no doubt burst out laughing at the 19th-century monument to him that dominates the square named in his honour. A close friend of his family lived in the patrician house at No 4. This was the heart of Roman Salzburg.

Walk towards the cathedral and into Residenzplatz.

9 Residenzplatz

The most magnificent square in Salzburg makes a suitable setting for the Residenz. Its spectacular Baroque fountain, the Residenzbrunnen, was added later. It is the largest Baroque fountain north of the Alps (1658–61). If you are in the square at 7am, 11am or 6pm, bells of the Glockenspiel will play for you as they have done without fail since 1702.

Traditional signs hanging in Getreidegasse

Gastein Valley and the Grossglockner Road

The Gastein Valley rises south of Salzburg, flanked by mountains and tributary valleys, through the canyons and waterfalls of Bad Gastein before ending dramatically against the north faces of the Austrian Alps. All along the valley, a glance in any direction reveals breathtaking views of weathered chalets perched atop mountain meadows against a backdrop of snow-covered granite peaks.

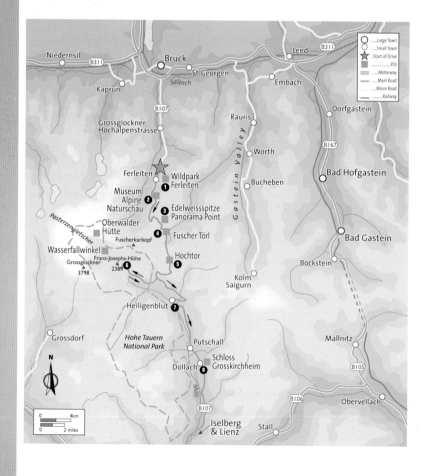

Niedernsil · B311 · Bruck · St Georgen · Lend · B311

Kaprun · Salzach · Embach

B107 · Rauris · Dorfgasten

Grossglockner Hochalpenstrasse · Wörth · B167

Ferleiten · Wildpark Ferleiten ❶ · Bucheben · Bad Hofgastein

Museum Alpine Naturschau ❷ · Edelweissspitze Panorama Point ❸ · Gastein Valley

Oberwalder Hütte · Fuscherkarkopf · Fuscher Törl ❹ · Bad Gastein

Pasterzengletscher · Wasserfallwinkel · Franz-Josephs-Höhe 2369 ❻ · Hochtor ❺ · Böckstein

Grossglockner 3798 · Kolm Saigurn

Heiligenblut ❼

Grossdorf · Hohe Tauern National Park · Putschall · Mallnitz

N · Döllach · Schloss Grosskirchheim ❽ · B105

Moll · B106 · Obervellach

0 — 4km · B107 · Iselberg & Lienz · Stall

0 — 2 miles

○ ...Large Town
◉ ...Small Town
★ ...Start of Drive
■ ...POI
▬ ...Motorway
▬ ...Main Road
▬ ...Minor Road
▬ ...Railway

View down the Gastein Valley

Gastein Valley

The Gastein Valley ranks with any in Austria for natural beauty and Alpine drama. Flat and fertile, this Austrian Shangri-La is only 40km (25 miles) long and isolated by surrounding mountains that reach glacial heights. Noble mountain valleys fan out from the valley floor like spokes from a wheel, making it an ideal base for hiking and skiing.

It is surrounded on three sides by central Europe's largest national park, Hohe Tauern (*see pp122–3*), where old-growth forests are refuge to rare wildlife and vegetation. A raging mountain stream, the Gasteiner Ache, cuts deep through bedrock to create a gorge. This is where the Tauern Tunnel was blasted through the rock in 1909, still the only way to enter by car or train. The Celts and Romans travelled through the

valley and perhaps even settled here in small numbers. A medieval gold rush brought great prosperity and a court (hof) at Bad Hofgastein and funded magnificent religious art.

The healing properties of the valley's thermal springs have attracted visitors throughout the ages, but this reached a height in the 19th century when European nobility, led by Austrian Emperor Franz Joseph, took the waters at Bad Gastein. In winter, the Gastein Valley is one of the biggest skiing areas in the province of Salzburg. The resorts of Bad Gastein, Bad Hofgastein and Dorfgastein have excellent ski runs; the whole region is covered by one ski pass.

Bad Gastein

This is a picture-postcard ski resort with thermal springs, a casino and *belle époque* hotels painted in the Imperial yellow of Vienna's Schönbrunn Palace. Johann Strauss and Franz Schubert both composed here. Bad Gastein is one of the three linked resorts in the valley, with the rustic village of Dorfgastein, and another spa town, Bad Hofgastein (*see opposite*).

Split in two by a waterfall, the town occupies a narrow gorge on the northern slope of the Sauern Alps. Seventeen thermal springs produce millions of litres of mineral-enriched water, bubbling up from deep under the ground and pumped into baths found throughout the resort. The Felsen Therme spa (*www. felsentherme.com*) is built around a mountain cave with a waterfall and natural outcrops. Indoor and outdoor pools are at 34°C (93°F). The main street is lined with hotels, luxury shops and quaint old buildings, while several promenades on the outskirts invite meditative walks with commanding views.

Bad Gastein has been a place to take the waters since at least the middle of the 14th century, but its glory years began when the prince-archbishop of Salzburg built a palace (Badeschloss) in 1793. By the second half of the 19th century, Bad Gastein was one of Europe's most famous spas. More than a few diplomatic documents were signed here between sips of mineral water, strolls along the Kaiser Wilhelm Promenade and evenings at the casino in the Grand Hotel de l'Europe. Those who prefer Gothic art to roulette can commune with the frescoes in the 14th-century St Nicholas' Church.

Bad Hofgastein

Bad Hofgastein occupies the widest and sunniest part of the valley at

The waterfall dividing Bad Gastein

The Felsentherme spa in Bad Gastein, hewn out of the rock

850m (2,789ft) above sea level. The cosy town centre is encircled by a wide pedestrian zone with many small shops, hotels and restaurants. The newly built congress and health centre is located in the middle of the town. The surrounding Kurpark has an extensive network of hiking trails. Bad Hofgastein offers a service supporting car-free holidays, with a 'mobility centre' that arranges transport in electric vehicles and bicycle hire.

Like its uphill neighbour, Bad Gastein, Bad Hofgastein is famous for its hot springs. The Alpen Therme (*www.alpentherme.com*) comes complete with geysers, three-storey water slides, a 'sauna world', and a sky bar with panoramic views of the mountains. The town also boasts Austria's first and only organic brewery (*www.schmaranz.at/english/kontakt.htm*).

In the 16th century, gold mining made Bad Hofgastein the second-richest town in Salzburg province after the capital. It was the proud seat of a court (Hof in der Gastein), and the 1560 Weitmoserschlössl, once the home of a wealthy mining family (and now a restaurant), dates from that time. The late Gothic Lady Church (1498) also owes its Gothic Madonna (designed by Fischer von Erlach) and fine Baroque altar (1738) to mineral wealth.

Böckstein

The most unusual spa in the Gastein Valley is in Böckstein: the Heilstollen (Healing Gallery) is located deep in an abandoned medieval gold mine.

The very special air contains radon. The inert gas is normally a health hazard, but this particular type of radon has an extremely short half-life. Inhaling it deep in the mountains is said to be therapeutic for the treatment of arthritis and other ailments. The waters of the Gastein Thermal Springs and the air of the Thermal Galleries are the only natural radon occurrences of this intensity in central Europe. You can learn more about the history of mining at the Böcksteiner Montanmuseum Hohe Tauern (Coal and Steel Museum, *Karl-Imhof-Ring 12. Open: May–Oct 10am–noon & 3–5.30pm. Admission charge*).

The village is popular with cross-country skiers, thanks to the 5km (3-mile) Böckstein trail, a circular course through the surrounding Alpine meadows. Böckstein's Baroque jewel is the Wallfahrtskirche Maria vom Guten Rat, a pilgrimage church built in 1766 with frescoes depicting medieval miners.

Dorfgastein

The town of Dorfgastein lies above the Gasteiner Klamm, where Gasteiner Ache roars through a gorge (the road to Dorfgastein gets there via a tunnel). Although it has some of the best skiing in the valley, Dorfgastein (population 1,400) has successfully maintained its rural character – horses and carts clatter past the church. Its castle, Burg Klammstein, is heavily restored and probably the oldest building in the Gastein Valley. It is now a restaurant that serves 'knights' meals'. The so-called 'Entrische church' is actually a spectacular cave that served as a shelter in the 16th century for Protestants on the run. Today, it is admired for its beautiful stalagmites (*Open: Guided tours Easter–end Sept 11am, noon, 2pm & 3pm; July & Aug hourly 10am–4pm. Closed: Mon*). Prehistoric human and animal (bear) remains were discovered in 1962. Para-scientists claim that the cave will cure you of headaches thanks to its healing force fields (said to be stronger than the ones in Lourdes, France).

The Grossglockner Road

The Grossglockner Hochalpenstrasse (High Alpine Road) crosses all the

---

SKIING IN THE GASTEIN VALLEY

Bad Gastein is one of the most popular ski resorts in Austria, with 250km (155 miles) of pistes. The longest run is 8km (5 miles). For cross-country skiers, there are 91km (57 miles) of Nordic tracks. The ski season runs from December to May, while February is normally the best month for snow conditions. You can ski from Bad Gastein to Bad Hofgastein, and return by train. Bad Hofgastein is the better choice for beginners, with an excellent network of nursery slopes. Dorfgastein has excellent intermediate and advanced pistes; it is linked to yet another huge ski domain called Grossarl by a 'ski circus'. All the Gastein Valley resorts belong to one ski pass, the Skiverbund Amade ski pass (*www.skiamade.com*), Austria's largest. It comprises 800km (497 miles) of slopes – all that on a single lift pass.

Gastein Valley and the Grossglockner Road

The Grossglockner Hochalpenstrasse

climatic and vegetation zones between Austria and the Arctic Circle. If it were a question of traversing latitude instead of altitude, this journey would require 4,000km (2,486 miles) of driving. The mother of all mountain roads also has the mother of all detours: the 'glacier road' leading to Franz-Josephs-Höhe – near Austria's highest peak and its largest glacier. At the northern end of the Hohe Tauern National Park (*see p122*), the Edelweissspitze Panorama offers the best 360-degree view of the Alps that can be reached (just) on four wheels.

There are glorious views of the Alps to be had …

The construction of the famous High Alpine Road was one of the most important events in modern Austrian history. Built in 1930–35 to create jobs during the depression, it was inaugurated in triumphal fashion. The government proclaimed it 'eternal evidence of Austrian achievement in the most difficult of times'. The Austrian President Wilhelm Miklas hailed it as 'proof of our will to survive' and added 'it will contribute to a meeting of hearts between the peoples of northern and southern Europe'. Democratic Austria, in building the road, was also expressing its defiance of Nazi Germany. Hitler had caused the near collapse of Austria's tourist industry by slapping a massive tax (1,000 Reichmarks) on Germans travelling to Austria. Few people could have imagined then that, in just three years, Austria would be part of the Third Reich. In the first year of the road's existence, 35,000 vehicles drove over it. Today, the figure is 1.5 million.

but the journey can be nerve-wracking!

Drive: Grossglockner Road

The drive is 136km (85 miles), plus 18km (11 miles) to reach Franz-Josephs-Höhe and 4km (2½ miles) to Edelweissspitze Panorama.

Allow 1 day.

See map on p78.

1 Wildpark Ferleiten

This point marks the northern entrance to the toll road. A toll attendant at the *Mauthaus* (toll booth) will politely demand a dizzying road-fee and hand over a map and pamphlet (the latter justifies the toll by citing high-altitude labour costs). The wildpark is a modest zoo in a magnificent setting. It has 200 animals (bears, wolves and lynx among others), and farm animals for the children to pet. If caged animals are not your thing, there is the **Rotmoos** swamp in the upper reaches of the valley – one of the most interesting in the entire Alps. Rare plants flourish in abundance there, including many varieties of the wide-leafed orchid that bloom in early summer. The Rotmoos moor is a 45-minute walk from the parking area at the Ferleiten toll booth.
Wildpark. Tel: 0654 62 20.
www.wildpark-ferleiten.at. Open:
8am–dusk. Tue–Sun there is a show
featuring birds of prey (July–Sept 11am & 3pm; Oct–June 3pm). Admission charge.

The route now follows the Fuscher Ache on the B107 up into Fuschertal, a deep, sparsely inhabited valley.

2 Museum Alpine Naturschau (Alpine Nature Museum)

This is a multimedia nature exhibition about local flora, fauna and ecology. None of it is state of the art, but it is still informative. A timeline plods through great moments in human history during the last millennium and points out that it can take an equal length of time for a high mountain meadow to form naturally.
Open: Summer. Free admission.
Continue on the B107 until you reach a left turn to Edelweissspitze. The winding road will take you up to the Panorama Point.

3 Edelweissspitze Panorama Point

Constructed in 1936, the stone tower (2,571m/8,435ft) is the highest point that you can reach by car from the

Grossglockner Road. This is a panorama encompassing 37 peaks over 3,000m (9,843ft) and 19 glaciers. Rare was the traveller who saw such a sight before the era of Alpine road building. One hundred million years ago this was all part of a vast predecessor to today's Mediterranean (Thethysmeer), when dinosaurs were at the top of the food chain.

Return to the B107 and turn left.

4 Fuscher Törl

The Fuscher Törl layby is famous for its glory-of-God views of Fuscherkarkopf and Sonnewelleck, and a dozen other peaks. A leading modern architect, Clemens Holzmeister, designed the pyramid-shaped chapel in memory of the 21 workers who lost their lives during the construction of the

Grossglockner Hochalpenstrasse. The stone roof echoes the peak of Sonnewelleck, which strongly resembles a pyramid. For one of the classic photographs of the Austrian Alps, align the chapel with the summit that inspired it.

5 Hochtor

The Grossglockner Road reaches its highest point (2,505m/8,219ft) at the north end of the Hochtor, part of a route that existed for many centuries before the modern road builders arrived.

Two objects found near the Hochtor have provided intriguing and unexplained glimpses into its early history: a Bronze Age (1700–1600 BC) dagger and a Celtic necklace (5th century BC). Road workers in the 1930s discovered a statuette of Hercules and the remains of a road,

The mountain hut at Edelweissspitze

Hochtor, the highest point of the Grossglockner

4km (2¹/₂ miles) wide in places, between Hochtor and Fuscher Törl. From the Middle Ages until the 17th century, this remote mountain pass was actually the third-most important commercial route over the Alps.

Take the Gletscherstrasse (Glacier Road) west through a series of hairpin turns. The road ends at an elevation of 2,369m (7,773ft) in a long terrace.

6 Franz-Josephs-Höhe

The Grossglockner massif (the highest mountain in Austria) rises above the terminus of the 9km (5¹/₂-mile) long Pasterzengletscher. The glacier is the number one destination for approximately 1.5 million people who use the Grossglockner Hochalpenstrasse (High Alpine Road) each year. In an earlier era, travellers

risked life and limb to see such a sight. A Gletscherbahn (funicular) descends 143m (469ft) from Freiwandeck. It no longer travels right to the edge of the glacier as it did when it was built in 1963. The glacier is relatively safe to walk on and, if time allows, an unforgettable hike (90 minutes' return journey) leads from the Freiwandeck parking area up the side of the Pasterze Glacier. Follow the signs for 'Oberwalder Hütte', and turn off on the Gamsgrubenweg, which climbs to the Wasserfallwinkel, a point with fine views of the glacier. The trail passes through a cirque that is covered with a layer of fine sand, up to 3m (10ft) thick, collected by the wind from the friable rock of the surrounding ridges, and rare cushion plants grow here. To find another one, you would have to

go to Central Asia or the Arctic Circle. Fit hikers will want to carry on all the way to the Oberwalder Hütte (2½ hours' return journey).
Return the way you came, back to the B107 and continue south.

7 Heiligenblut

Heiligenblut is one of the most scenic villages in Austria and a popular point from which to enter the Hohe Tauern National Park (*see pp122–3*). The 15th-century Heiligenblutkirche (Holy Blood Church) was venerated in the Middle Ages and pilgrims came in great numbers to catch sight of its holiest relic: a tiny phial of Jesus' blood. The village has ski runs on the peaks of the Schareck (2,604m/8,544ft) and the Gjaidtroghöhe (2,969m/9,741ft). Below Heiligenblut is the entrance to Gössnitz Valley and an 80m (262ft) waterfall, the Gössnitzfall.

8 Döllach

The village of Döllach is embedded in the upper Mölltal Valley, surrounded by the remote peaks of the Hohe Tauern. It is a relaxed point of departure for excursions into Hohe Tauern National Park and a family-oriented ski resort. The Goldbergbau und Heimatmuseum has exhibits related to the region's medieval gold rush in a 16th-century castle – the Schloss Grosskirchheim.
Take the road south towards Lienz. The road traverses a classic Almlandschaft (mountain farmscape). Many farmhouses still have shingle roofs and fences woven from laths. The descent to Iselberg is best interrupted on one of the first two loops – both have majestic views of the Dolomites. The upper valley of the Drava is visible curving southwest around Lienz.

Snowy peaks near Franz-Josephs-Höhe

Drive: Grossglockner Road

The disappearing glaciers

The disappearing Alpine glaciers are startling evidence of climate change. Glaciers have been described as the canary in the mine for global warming studies: the oldest ones have been around for 10,000 years; the youngest for only 50 years. Scientists say their rapid disappearance will cause havoc in the future.

It is estimated that the European Alps have already lost one-third of their glaciers in the past century.

Researchers at Zurich University estimate that the glaciers in the Alps lost up to one-tenth of their volume in the hot 2003 summer alone. An increase in temperature of 3°C, the same study cautions, could cause another 80 per cent of glacial ice to disappear at some point before the end of the century. If it goes as high as 5°C, the Alps might not have a single glacier left in 2100. These gloomy forecasts

Austria's glaciers are shrinking at an alarming rate

Viewing terrace for the glacier at Grossglockner

are based on temperature projections from the Intergovernmental Panel on Climate Change (IPCC).

During the early 1900s, the Pasterzengletscher (Pasterze Glacier), Austria's largest (covering an area of 20sq km/8 sq miles), was much larger than it is now, reaching as far as the Margaritzen reservoir further down the valley. This made the Glocknerhaus mountain lodge a convenient place for assaults on the Grossglockner summit. The retreating glacier loses about 5m (16ft) in height and 20m (66ft) in length per year.

A novel effort is being made to save at least one Austrian glacier. In the Tyrol, scientists are trying to stop the Stubai Glacier from melting by covering parts of it with a sun-reflecting 'blanket' to prevent summer melt. The technique, while promising, is far too expensive in labour and materials to save entire glaciers.

Winter sports are vital to the Austrian economy – 'white gold' has made once remote and impoverished villages rich. Yet the consequences go far beyond a loss of tourist revenue. It represents a fundamental change in the country's ecosystem. Glaciers feed mountain water supplies, and, without them, towns will face water shortages. In some areas, glacial runoff is vital to power production. Glacier scientists and businesses are now struggling to calculate what the costs of global warming will be to Austria, and what, if anything, can be done about it.

Salzkammergut

The word 'Salzkammer' has no geographic or political meaning. It is a reminder of the days when the mountains belonged to the clerical state of Salzburg. The salt-rich region was managed by the treasury (Kammer). The prince-archbishops of Salzburg received a big cut of the profits and soared towards the top of medieval Europe's list of richest men. Prince-archbishop Wolf Dietrich von Raitenau used the money to finance the construction of Salzburg's Baroque city centre.

The fjord-like scenery is dotted with 76 turquoise lakes, and contains the rugged Dachstein and Totes Gebirge ranges, small historic towns, lakeside villages, ice caves and salt mines. Today, the region lies mostly within Upper Austria, but it also reaches into the provinces of Salzburg (Wolfgangsee and Fuschlsee) and Styria (Aussee).

Austrian royals, politicians, poets and painters used to descend on this region in droves, and it inspired music by Brahms, Mahler and Wagner.

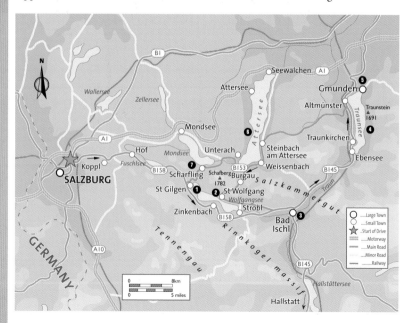

There are many opportunities to leave the car behind here. Steamers connect the villages on the larger lakes, a cogwheel train and cable cars ascend the peaks and, for the more energetic, cycling paths skirt the gentler lake shores. There is also an extensive network of trails and mountain-bike routes. The Salzkammergut is at its most charming just before or after the summer and during winter.

Sculpture by the waterfront, Gmunden

Hallstatt

Hallstättersee is a strong competitor for the world's most beautiful lake, and Hallstatt for the most beautiful lakeside village. While composing *Parsifal* here, Wagner immortalised the Dachstein mountains as the 'Kingdom of the Grail'.

The town is squeezed between the Salzberg (Salt Mountain) – part of the Dachstein range – and Hallstättersee, a deep lake (8km/5 miles long by 2km/1¼ miles wide). For most of its history, the only way to Hallstatt was on foot or by boat. When the railway was built, the only space for a station was on the far shore. A boat meets every train, and as you skim across to Hallstatt, the ethereal character of the place is revealed. A 1966 road blasted through the mountain has made way for day-trippers, but most of them don't stay for very long.

Hallstatt has an odd collection of houses, some of them are from the 16th and 17th centuries. They are piled one above the other, higgledy-piggledy, on the narrow terraces wedged between the lake and the slopes of Salzberg. From the mountain above, the enormous Mühlbach waterfall plunges into the centre of the village near its market square.

The Maria Himmelfahrt Church overlooks the lake and village and is reached by a long, old, covered wooden

The picturesque village of Hallstatt …

... and the equally gorgeous lake beside it

flight of steps. Its faded St Christopher on its outer wall welcomes all travellers. In the harmonious interior a late-Gothic altar depicts Mary and, in the wings, St Barbara, the patron saint of miners, and St Catherine, the patron saint of woodcutters. Deceased villagers are interred, temporarily, on the terrace surrounding the church. After their ten-year 'lease' is up, the bones of the dead are added to the collection at the nearby Beinhaus (ossuary). The bones of the ancestors of the present inhabitants of Hallstatt are stacked there neatly, many painted with oak leaves, iron crosses and roses. Some are centuries old, others quite recent.

Only a few kilometres south of Hallstatt are the magnificent Dachstein ice and limestone caves (*www.dachstein.at*). The Rieseneishöhle ('ice cave') – the third largest in the world – offers the most remarkable sight of frozen rivers and waterfalls. The Mammuthöhle ('mammoth cave') is a series of limestones caverns formed by an ancient underground river. In the Koppenbrüller Cave, a waterfall and geyser compete for attention with the stalactites.

Drive: Salzkammergut lakes

The tour takes in the three large lakes that form the heart of the Salzkammergut: Attersee, the Mondsee and the Wolfgangsee.

Allow 2–3 days.

See map on p92.

From Salzburg, take the scenic B158 to St Gilgen.

1 St Gilgen

The town of St Gilgen lies on Lake Wolfgang, which heats up to 24°C (75°F) in summer and freezes over in front of the town during winter. Tourism and water sports, including an 1873 steamship line, are the town's main source of income. Mozart's mother was born here, a fact memorialised on a plaque in the town's central square. Mozart's beloved sister Nannerl also lived here after her marriage. In the interwar years, many of Austria's most important painters created an art colony in the nearby village of Zinkenbach. It was dispersed in 1939 under pressure from the Nazis.

2 St Wolfgang

St Wolfgang is a summer paradise on the lake of the same name. An antique cog railway chugs up to the summit of Schafberg at 1,782m (5,847ft) for a panoramic view. The 15th-century Pilgrim's Church possesses several artistic treasures: the altar by Michael Pacher, one of the glories of Gothic art in Austria; the Baroque Schwanthaler altar; and an *Ecce Homo* by Meinrad Guggenbichler.

Take the direct road to Bad Ischl (not the one through Strobl).

3 Bad Ischl

Bad Ischl is on a peninsula that lies between the River Traun and its tributary the Ischl. It was the summer residence of Emperor Franz Joseph I (1830–1916), and the town's architectural style is that of the old Austro-Hungarian monarchy. The emperor's Imperial Villa is now a museum (his great-grandchild and family live in the left wing) full of art and hunting trophies. You can see the desk where, on a hot summer's day in 1914, he signed the declaration of war on Serbia, setting in motion the carnage of World War I and the end of Habsburg rule. The town also has several spas and a pastry shop founded by Herr Zauner, the former baker to the imperial court.

Go north on the B145, following the Traun River between the Hollengebirge and Totes Gebirge ranges, then continue along the west shore of the Traunsee.

4 Traunsee

At almost 200m (656ft), Traunsee is the deepest lake in Austria. The cliff road from Ebensee to Traunkirchen is hewn directly into the rock overlooking the lake. Traunkirchen has a population of 1,500 and is situated on a peninsula. It is a former Benedictine nunnery reincarnated as a summer resort. The early Baroque parish church has a curious 'fisherman's pulpit' in the form of a boat, complete with oars and fishing nets (1753).

5 Gmunden

On the north side of Traunsee, Gmunden is located on the Traun River, at the point where it flows out of the lake of the same name. The historic town has a brace of castles and a spa. The parish church of the Assumption, originally Gothic, was remodelled in Baroque style in the 18th century. The astonishing Rathaus (Town Hall) is equipped with arcades, loggias and a ceramic carillon. The late-Gothic Kammerhof houses the Municipal Museum, with rooms devoted to Brahms and local history. If you want to get married, head straight for the island Castle Orth. The venerable *Schloss* now specialises in weddings. Rippled-green ceramic pottery has been a tradition here for more than 350 years.

River Traun, Bad Ischl

Drive: Salzkammergut lakes

Between Unterach and Weissenbach, a road veers off to Burgau (6km/3¾ miles). From there, a 30-minute walk leads to the Burggrabenklamm, one of the most spectacular gorges in Austria.

You can cruise the lake on the *Gisela*, which claims to be the world's oldest coal-fired paddle steamer, or take a ride on Austria's oldest (1894) and steepest (10 per cent grade) streetcar, followed by a lift in Austria's oldest operational cable car, the Grünbergseilbahn, to the top of Traunstein mountain (1,691m/ 5,548ft). The view takes in Gmunden's esplanade, Castle Orth, Traunsee and three mountain peaks – Traunstein, Hochkogel and Eriakogel – which form,

locals say, the silhouette of a *Schlafende Griechin* (sleeping Greek girl).
Take the Bad Ischl road south to Altmünster, then follow signs for Attersee.

6 Attersee

The Attersee is Austria's largest lake. The town of the same name on the other side of the lake is a centre for sailing, with a shipyard and an important yacht club that organises international sailing competitions. Gustav Mahler composed prolifically here at Attersee – you can visit his former summerhouse in the village of Steinbach. You can also see the former home of Gustav Klimt in Seewalchen.
Tour around the southern end of the

Gmunden seen from Traunsee

Mondsee is sheltered by the surrounding mountains

lake, calling into Weissenbach village on the southeastern shore of the lake, and take route B153 west to Mondsee.

7 Mondsee

This sickle-shaped 'moon' lake heats up in summer and is popular for swimming and other water sports, such as windsurfing and sailing. The lake is set picturesquely against the backdrop of Schafberg and the cliff-faced Drachenwand. Apart from the modest town of Mondsee and a few scattered hotels and country houses, not many people live here. The town of Mondsee is renowned for its parish church, Gothic on the outside, Baroque on the inside.

The B153 crosses a pass between Scharfling and St Gilgen with views of the Wolfgangsee and the Rinnkogel massif. Descend to St Gilgen and return to Salzburg via the B158.

Bad Ischl
Kaiservilla. *Tel: 0613 22 32 41. www.kaiservilla.at. Open: May–mid-Oct 9.30am–4.45pm. Admission charge.*

Schafbergbahn steam rack railway/Wolfgangsee boat trip
www.schafbergbahn.at

Traunsee boat trip
www.traunseeschiffahrt.at

Wolfgangsee boat trip
www.rundfahrten.at

Salt mines

'Hall' was one of the most important words in the Celtic language – it meant salt.

The Celts living in Hallstatt traded salt from the Baltic to the Mediterranean, creating an entire civilisation in the process. In fact, Hallstatt has given its name to a period of human history. Archaeologists refer to the 8th to 4th centuries BC as the 'Hallstatt Age'. It was in this period that the Celtic tribes arrived from the east and the early Iron Age began.

The world's oldest salt mine – the evidence of salt mining goes back to the Neolithic era – runs through the heart of Salzberg mountain above Hallstatt. Tourists have been visiting its dark underworld since the 19th century. There are tours from April to October. Despite the theme-park atmosphere, it is still a working salt mine. A steep funicular ride whisks you to the mine entrance with fabulous views over Lake Hallstatt, followed by a 15-minute walk to the entrance.

In the early Middle Ages, salt was carved out of the mountain in the shape of hearts. These 'Hallstatt hearts' were transported down the mountain in leather backpacks. Beginning in the 12th century, the rocks of salt were dissolved in pits of water; the saline solution was then carried by pipes down the mountain. This pipeline was extended in 1595 to Ebensee. The builders hollowed out 13,000 trees to construct the 40km (25-mile) long conduit; it is considered to have been the world's first industrial pipeline.

In 1846, miners discovered a necropolis that was eventually found to contain several thousand prehistoric graves. The finds included exquisite gold jewellery, weapons, bronze and ceramic vessels and finely wrought iron tools.

HALLSTATT MUSEUM

Seestrasse 56. Tel: 6134 82 80 15. www.museum-hallstatt.at. Open: May–Sept 9am–6pm, shorter hours in winter. Closed: winter Mon–Wed. Admission charge.

SALZWELTEN HALLSTATT

Salzbergstrasse 21. www.salzwelten.at. Open: end Apr–mid-Sept 9.30am–4.30pm; mid-Sept–end Sept 9.30am–3.30pm; Oct 9.30am–3pm. Admission charge.

Salt crystals at the museum in Hallstatt

Hallstatt's local museum offers an overview of the region's geological and human history as well as the town's 7,000 years of salt mining (exhibits are in German, but an English text is available). Hallstatt's most valuable treasures now belong to the Natural History Museum in Vienna, but a selection of them is on loan to Hallstatt's local museum.

Tyrol

The word 'Tyrol' first crops up in 1271. Before that, the region was simply called the 'Land in the Mountains'. It stretches from its highest peak – the Wildspitze (3,774m/12,382ft) – in the southwest to the Wilder Kaiser Mountains in the northeast, and from the Lienzer Dolomiten in the southeast to Jungholz, a mountain enclave. In between are the Stubai, Pitz, Ötztal, Ziller and Kitzbühel Alps.

The wide valley of the Inn sweeps through the Tyrol's entire east–west length. Since time immemorial, the Inn Valley has been the crossroads between Southern and Northern Europe.

Germany and the Tyrol share the

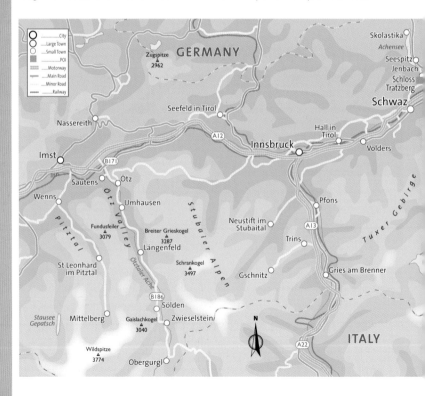

Zugspitze (2,962m/9,718ft), officially the highest mountain in Germany.

The region historically known as the Tyrol was larger than it is today. Southern Tyrol was invaded by Italy during World War I, and the 1919 Treaty of Versailles ratified its annexation. Two pieces of the province remained within the newly created Austrian Republic – North and East Tyrol – with no common border. Rhäto-romansh, a dialect of Latin, remained a living language for centuries in the remoter parts of the Tyrol. Today, it is still spoken in a few southern Tyrolean villages. The

discovery of a well-preserved Stone Age man in 1991 on a Tyrolean mountain pass reveals much about the earliest human history in the region.

INNSBRUCK

The political and cultural capital of the Tyrol, Innsbruck never lets you forget that you are in the heart of the Alps. Thanks to its strategic position at the foot of the Brenner Pass – the lowest through the Alps – the city prospered as a crossroads between south and north, Italy and Germany. Emperor Maximilian I made the provincial town the centre of the Habsburg Empire in

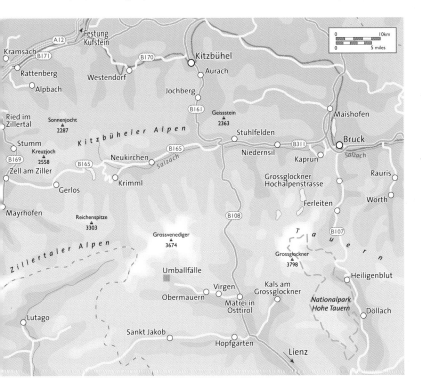

the 1490s. Today, Innsbruck's rare synergy between city and nature, like the Alps themselves, is endangered by overdevelopment.

Alpenzoo (Alpine Zoo)

This is the highest zoo in Europe and a breathtakingly beautiful place to observe 2,000 Alpine animals that represent 150 endangered species. There are also rare species of Alpine fish in specially designed aquariums. *Entrance in the Weiherburggasse or via the celebrated Iraqi architect Zaha Hadid's new Hungerburgbahn funicular. Tel: 0512 29 23 23. www.alpenzoo.at. Open: summer 9am–6pm; winter 9am–5pm. Admission charge.*

Domkirche St Jakob (St James' Cathedral)

The Baroque cathedral was built between 1717 and 1724. The Asam brothers (Cosmas Damian, the painter, and Egid Quirin, the stucco worker) decorated the dome ceilings. The Tomb

The Silver Chapel at the Hofkirche

of Archduke Maximilian III, built by Caspar Gras in 1620, is of a Grandmaster of the Teutonic Order (not the same man who was emperor of Austria). The beautiful *Gnadenbild Mariahilfe* (*Our Lady of Succour*, 1537) by Lucas Cranach the Elder occupies the high altar. Traditionally, mothers came to *Gnadenbild Mariahilfe* after giving birth to pray for the survival of their infants. It became the most widely copied portrait of the Virgin Mary in the Tyrol. *Domplatz 6. Tel: 0512 58 39 02. Open: Mon–Sat 7.30am–6.30pm, Sun 8am–6.30pm. Free admission.*

Goldenes Dachl (Golden Roof)

The 'Golden Roof' is Innsbruck's most famous landmark and perhaps the most beautiful balcony in Europe. Maximilian I used to sit in the Gothic oriel while tournaments and courtly spectacles were held in the square below. Light winks off its 2,600 gilt copper roof tiles, and Maximilian I is ever present as a fresco in the company of his two wives – the one he loved, Maria von Burgundy, and the unfortunate Maria Bianca Sforza whom he married for territory and used as security for his drinking debts. Inside, there is a small museum and gift shop, the Maximilianeum, with 11 exhibits devoted to the life of Maximilian I. *Herzog-Friedrich-Strasse 15. Tel: 0512 58 11 11. www.goldenes-dachl.at. Open: May–Sept daily 10am–5pm; Oct–Apr Tue–Sun 10am–5pm. Closed: Nov. Admission charge.*

Innsbruck, at the bottom of the Brenner Pass

Hofburg

The Hofburg looks much today as it did in 1743 when the Empress Maria Theresa had it rebuilt in the latest Baroque fashion after an earthquake. She loved yellow, and yellow it has been ever since. By far the most impressive room is the Riesensaal, with ceiling frescoes by F A Maulbertsch and full-length portraits of the imperial family, including a soft and tender Marie Antoinette.
Rennweg 1. Tel: 0512 58 71 86. www.hofburg-innsbruck.at. Open: 9am–5pm. Admission charge.

Hofkirche

The church was built (1553–63) under Ferdinand I to house Europe's most famous tomb, the Grabdenkmal Kaiser Maximilian I. The tomb was intended as a monument to Kaiser Maximilian I and, at the same time, the entire line – real and imagined – of the Kaiser (Holy Roman Emperors). The kneeling figure of Maximilian I is surrounded by marble reliefs depicting the marriages, wars and diplomatic triumphs of his reign. The tomb is flanked by 28 larger-than-life bronze statues created by an unprecedented team of artists, sculptors and metalworkers during half a century. In sharp contrast to these 'black men' figures, as they are called by Innsbruckers, is the tomb of Andreas Hofer, the national hero of the Tyrol (*see p107*). The tomb is of the purest white marble, located to the right as you enter. The upstairs Silberne Kapelle (Silver Chapel) – built so that a nobleman and common woman could lay together – bears witness to the most famous love story in Tyrolean history. Archduke Ferdinand chose love over power and married a commoner, Philippine Welser. The life-size figures of Ferdinand and Philippine were carved by the same sculptor who made Maximilian I's statue, Alexandre Colin. The name of the chapel refers to the huge embossed silver Madonna.

The 16th-century Schloss Ambras is Tyrol's largest castle

*Universitätsstrasse 2. Tel: 0512 58 43 02.
www.hofkirche.at. Open: Mon–Sat
9am–5pm, Sun 12.30–5pm;
summer until 5.30pm.*

Maria-Theresien-Strasse

This stately Baroque boulevard
overwhelms with grand architectural
gestures that nevertheless pale in
stature beneath the north face of the
Karwendel Mountains. The Annasäule
(St Anne's Column), which marks the
halfway point, commemorates the
retreat of Bavarian troops at the end
of the Spanish War of Succession.
The Palais Lodron (*No 11*) hides two
Gothic houses joined behind a fancy
rococo façade. No 10 has been the
Jugendstil building since 1909. The
Palais Toryer-Spaur (*No 39*) has a lavish
stucco façade and an oriel typical for
17th-century Innsbruck. The Altes
Landhaus (*No 43*) is one of the Tyrol's
finest surviving patrician residences
from the Baroque period. The Palais
Trapp-Wolkenstein (*No 38*) and Palais
Fugger-Taxis (*No 45*) across the street
are flashy 17th-century palaces built
with Italianate flourishes.

Schloss Ambras

Archduke Ferdinand (1529–95) built
Tyrol's largest castle, Ambras, for his
wife, Philippine Welser (*see* Silberne
Kapelle *p105*), who rewarded him
with lavishly prepared feasts that she
described in a cookbook still important
to Austrian cuisine. The Rüstungssäle
in the lower part of the castle provides

a formidable spectacle of jousting
mannequins and medieval arms and
armour. The highlight of the upper
castle is the Renaissance Spanischer
Saal (Spanish room), with a wooden
inlaid ceiling, frescoes of Tyrolean
nobility and a great gallery of
Habsburg family portraits.
*Schlossstrasse 20. Tel: 0525 24 48 02.
www.khm.at/ambras. Open: 10am–5pm;
Aug until 7pm. Closed: Nov.
Admission charge.*

Tiroler Volkskunstmuseum

This museum of popular art occupies a
16th-century cloister with a fine series
of Renaissance arcades. Its unrivalled
collection of Alpine folklore includes
furniture, costumes, farm tools,
carnival masks, Christmas Nativity
scenes and hope chests.
*Universitätsstrasse 2. Tel: 0512 59 48 95
10. www.tiroler-volkskunstmuseum.at.
Open: Mon–Sat 9am–5pm, Sun
10am–5pm; summer until 5.30pm.*

ANDREAS HOFER

Andreas Hofer (1767–1810) is the national
hero of the Tyrol and the subject of the
Tyrolean anthem. He was an innkeeper, wine
and cattle merchant, and born leader of men.
Against almost impossible odds, he briefly
liberated the Tyrol (1809–10) from an
occupation force of Bavarian and Napoléonic
troops. In his lifetime, he was the object of
hero worship by the common people and the
court ladies of Vienna. He was a man of action,
not words: 'Männer s'isch Zeit' ('Men, it is
time') he said before his most famous battle at
Bergisel, above Innsbruck (now the site of the
Olympic ski jump designed by Zaha Hadid).

LOWER INN VALLEY

The lower valley of the Inn River forms a flat, green trough across the Tyrol. The province's mountainous geography has dictated the concentration of commerce and population here. The Inn Valley *Autobahn* – one of central Europe's main traffic arteries – covers the distance between Innsbruck and Kufstein in 40 minutes unless it is clogged by lorries and tourists. People who prefer travel to transit, however, will find that the valley's byways lead to scenery as beautiful as any in the Alps, dotted with castles and castle ruins, medieval towns, monasteries and idyllic villages.

Achensee

The fjord-like Achensee, wedged between the Karwendel and Rofan mountain ranges, was born in the last ice age and is nicknamed Tyrol's 'blue eye'. It is far too cold to swim in, but people have fun doing things on top of the water like sailing and windsurfing. Ferry boats cross the lake from Seespitz to Skolastika and back (about an hour each way). The *Dampf-Zahnradbahn* (steam cog-railway) is the oldest train of its kind in the world still in operation. For more than 100 years, it has linked Jenbach with the shore of the Achensee. The 7km (4-mile) ride is an impressive trip into the mountains of Tyrol with a maximum gradient of 16 per cent; it takes you directly to a ship landing pier in Seespitz (*Tel: 05244 22 43. www.achenseebahn.at*).

Fortress Kufstein (Festung Kufstein)

Kufstein lies on the Inn River, almost on the border of Germany between the Kaiser Mountains and the Bavarian Alps. It was strategically important to

The clear blue waters of Achensee

Festung Kufstein, up above the Inn River

Bavaria until 1504 when it was ceded to the Austrians. The area covered by the Festung Kufstein is larger than the entire historic town centre of Kufstein; in places it has walls almost 5m (16ft) thick. The fortress now houses a Heimatmuseum. Its Burgturm (Keep) contains the mighty 1931 Heldenorgel (Heroes Organ) that was built as a memorial to German and Austrian soldiers who died in World War I. Two songs are played on it every day at noon (also at 6pm in summer).
Tel: 05372 60 23 50.
www.festung.kufstein.at. Open:
9am–5pm. Museum open: 9am–5pm,
winter until 4pm. Admission charge.

Hall in Tirol

Hall is the Tyrol's best-preserved medieval city. The original source of its wealth was salt, which was already being mined by Celts when the Romans arrived. The most important city in the northern Tyrol until the 15th century, it was then eclipsed by rival Innsbruck. Its Altstadt (Old Town) is the largest ensemble of historic buildings in the Tyrol. The Burg Hassegg once guarded the river trade in salt. Its polygonal tower, the Münzerturm, is the city's most famous landmark, and climbing it is the best way to get to know the lie of the surrounding land. The Pfarrkirche St Nikolaus is another impressive reminder of the city's former wealth and importance, and one of the strangest churches in Austria. The choir is crooked because the church rests on a cliff and could not be enlarged equally in both directions. The city's oldest church, the diminutive Romanesque

Magdalenenkapelle, lurks behind St Nikolaus. It has a not-to-be-missed fresco of the Last Judgement with a motley cast of medieval characters, and it does double duty as a war memorial. The Bergbaumuseum is a reconstructed salt mine with an intriguing series of pits and shafts and a long, slippery wooden slide. It is not as impressive as the ones in Schwaz or Hallstatt (*see p94*), but there are no queues to get in, either.

Karlskirche

One of the most fanciful Baroque buildings in the Tyrol, Karlskirche in Volders was designed by a 17th-century doctor and biologist, Hippolytus Guarinoni (1571–1654), a resident of nearby Hall. Guarinoni dedicated it to Karl Borromäus, a religious zealot and headstrong leader of the Counter-Reformation. Later generations added side chapels, and the noted Baroque artist Martin Knoller painted the cupolas and the high altar in 1765. Unfortunately, the engineers of the *Autobahn* placed their speedway next to the church.
Volderwaldstrasse 3, Volders.
Tel: 05223 46 08 4.

Rattenberg

Crushed against a cliff on the south shore of the Inn River, Rattenberg seems to be clinging to the Middle Ages. The town has some notable Renaissance houses, many adorned with frescoes and oriels with lead-paned windows. The hillside church, Pfarrkirche St Virgil, has two naves and two altars so that merchants and miners could hold Masses

In the courtyard of Schloss Tratzberg

separately. It is also the site of the ruined Burg Rattenberg where a plaque commemorates a righteous Chancellor named Wilhelm Biener who was beheaded after a rigged trial in 1651. Plays about his life are sometimes performed in the castle's open-air theatre.

Schloss Tratzberg

This castle was built as a fortress against the Bavarians in the 13th century, but was transformed centuries later by wealthy families (the Tänzls, Illsungs and Fuggers) with interests in the silver mines of Schwaz. They were more interested in graceful living than impregnable defence. It is the only castle in the Tyrol whose period decoration is intact. The intricately carved wood panelling, heavy furniture, inlaid chests and canopied beds would make you feel right at home if you were wealthy and living in the Renaissance. *3km (2 miles) west of Jenbach. Tel: 05242 63 56 6. www.schloss-tratzberg.at. Open: hour-long tours mid-Mar–Oct 10am–4pm, every half hour. Admission charge.*

Schwaz

Although its origins as a city go back to the first millennium, Schwaz began its golden age in 1400 when it experienced a massive economic boom due to its silver mines, which employed 10,000 miners. Its immense wealth financed the wars and diplomacy of Maximilian I and the expansion of the Habsburg Empire. The cavernous Pfarrkirche zu

Schwaz was known for the success of its silver mines

Unserer Lieben Frau is the largest Gothic hall-church in the Tyrol. Yet the highlight for many tourists is the Schau Silberbergwerk – a mine converted into a highly atmospheric museum. The 90-minute guided tour begins by putting on a miner's helmet and overcoat and includes mini-train rides and a trip down a slide.

EMPEROR MAXIMILIAN I

Kaiser Maximilian I (Tyroleans call him Kaiser Max) was the last German emperor to lead his troops personally into battle, hence his epithet of 'The Last Knight'. Historians, however, would later regard him as the first 'Renaissance man' to sit on an emperor's throne because of his patronage of the arts, interest in science and skill in harnessing the forces of change to reshape Europe. His ghost is ubiquitous in the Inn Valley. Maximilian was the first European ruler to realise the importance of public relations and, centuries later, you still feel his influence. Even in remote mountain valleys and on the shores of high Alpine lakes, locals tirelessly remind you that Kaiser Max hunted and fished there.

Drive: Kitzbühel and Ziller valleys

The Kitzbühel and Ziller valleys sum up all the extremes of the Tyrol, from Alpine grandeur to tourist tackiness, folklore to kitsch, and trendiness to wilderness.

The route is 94km (58 miles).

Allow 1 day, but it would make an ideal long weekend.

1 Kitzbühel

The origins of Kitzbühel are in the Bronze Age. In the Middle Ages, it benefited from its position on a trade route between Munich and Venice. However, by the turn of the 19th century it was just another mining town, although with a medieval centre, when a delivery of skis arrived from Norway. It has since become one of the world centres of skiing, particularly during the annual Hahnenkamm downhill race – the most exciting event in the World Cup calendar. Its historic centre, crammed with chic boutiques, has two interesting monuments – the graceful, late Gothic church, Pfarrkirche St Andreas (the interior is Baroque), and its hilltop companion, the Liebfrauenkirche.

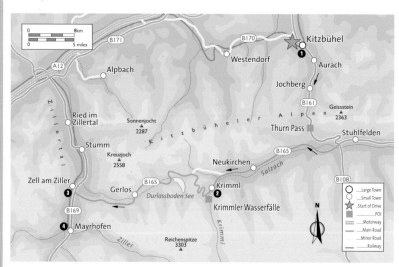

Take the B161 south to the mountain pass of Thurn, which marks the border with the province of Salzburg. Turn right onto the B165 going west to Krimml and enjoy the pastoral scenery of the broad Salzach Valley.

2 Krimmler Wasserfälle (Krimmler Waterfalls)

The Krimmler Waterfalls are among the most impressive in Europe (and the sixth highest in the world). The quantity of water is at its greatest on early afternoons in July and August when the sun is hottest on the glaciers above. At the top of the falls, there is an inn, the Krimmler Tauernhaus, that first opened its doors in 1437.

Continue on the B165 past Durlassboden See and Gerlos to Zell am Ziller. The road executes a well-engineered downward spiral with fine views of the Ziller Valley.

GAUDERFEST

First celebrated over 400 years ago, the spring festival in Zell am Ziller (*1 & 2 May*) re-enacts medieval events that once took place on the Gauderlehen (a meadow belonging to the local brewery). Would-be local heroes engage in Tyrolean-style wrestling, and rams are paired off for the *Widderstossen*, or 'Butting of Heads'. There is plenty of brass music, food (spicy beef sausages called *Gauderwürsten*) and the Cyclops-strength *Gauderbock*, a brew that makes even strong men faint. The high point is the Gauderfestzug – a parade of hundreds of villagers and local militia in *Trachten* (folk costumes) accompanied by local lads shaking bells to 'wake up' the natural world from its winter sleep.

ZILLERTAL RAILWAY

The Zillertal railway has been in operation since 1902. Diesel trains run on the hour in summer between Mayrhofen and Achensee, and steam trains puff back and forth twice a day. For a fee, passengers are allowed to operate the train. A train ride can be combined with a lake cruise on Achensee or a hike.

Zillertaler Verkehrsbetriebe, Jenbach. Tel: 05244 60 60. www.zillertalbahn.at

3 Zell am Ziller

The name Zell am Ziller probably refers to monks who lived in the area in the 9th century – missionaries sent by Salzburg's sainted bishops Rupert and Virgil. After a severe flood, Empress Maria Theresa helped the town by building the Baroque church, Pfarrkirche St Veit, which has the largest dome in the Tyrol and a Greek cross floor plan, surrounded by chapels. The most famous Tyrolean festival, the Gauderfest, takes place in Zell each May.

Turn left (south) on the B169.

4 Mayrhofen

The town of Mayrhofen, one of the most popular ski resorts in the Alps, lies at the end of the Ziller Valley where four side valleys branch off into the Zillertal Alps – the Zemmgrund, Zillergrund, Stilluptal and Tux valleys. Mayrhofen recently joined with the resorts of Hippach, Finkenberg and Tux to form the Zillertal3000, an area that provides more than 146km (90 miles) of trails and is serviced by 46 lifts.

The oldest European

On 19 September 1991, German hikers from Nuremberg were shocked to find a corpse on the Similaun Glacier in the Ötztal Alps. When the police arrived, their suspicions were heightened by the discovery of an axe. The famous mountain climber Reinhold Messner happened to be in the area. He came to examine the corpse and declared that it was 'more than a hundred years old'.

In fact, the body was 5,300 years old. Austrian authorities recovered the corpse but surveys showed that the body had been found a few metres inside Italian territory. Europe's oldest natural human mummy is now on display at the South Tyrol Museum of Archaeology in Bolzano, Italy. Scientists have studied 'Ötzi'– the nickname comes from Ötztal, the region in which he was discovered – intensively for over a decade.

Physiologically, Ötzi was no different from a modern human being. At the time of his death, he was over 30 and suffering from parasites, arthritis and athlete's foot. He had about 57 tattoos, and claims have been made that he used

Ötztal, where Ötzi was found

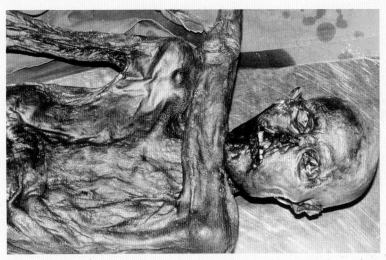

The man himself – Ötzi is now residing in Italy

acupuncture. Scientists have examined Ötzi's dental enamel, bones and minerals, comparing them with water and soils in the region. They believe he was born in the Italian South Tyrol village of Feldthurns, only 60km (37 miles) from the spot where he died. An arrowhead wound in his left shoulder suggests that Ötzi was murdered, either by bandits or in a boundary dispute. He might also have been with a companion. DNA analysis found the blood of several individuals on the arrowhead, and on Ötzi's knife and coat.

Ötzi was well armed with a copper axe, flint knife, longbow and arrows. He was wearing a woven grass cloak and leather vest, and waterproof shoes made from bearskin, deer hide and tree bark. Ötzi had tools to repair his weapons and clothing, as well as flint and pyrite for creating sparks. His most astonishing possession was a first-aid kit that included a dozen different plants and a species of mushroom known to have antibacterial properties.

The German tourist who discovered the mummy, Helmut Simon, aged 67, fell to his death during a freak blizzard not far from the spot where he found Ötzi. His fate, and that of several other people who died unexpectedly – all of them somehow associated with Ötzi – inspired claims of a 'mummy's curse'. Scientific research on Europe's oldest natural human mummy continues, and, curse or no curse, Ötzi still has much to reveal.

Drive: Ötz Valley

The Ötz Valley is the longest tributary valley of the Inn, with the highest peak in north Tyrol and the highest village in Austria. Glaciers cover 200sq km (77 sq miles) of it.

It is 48km (30 miles) to the end of the Ötz Valley.

Allow at least half a day.

The Ötz Valley is clearly signposted from the Inn Valley Autobahn and the B171.

1 Ötz

Ötz is the town that gave the Ötz Valley its name. Sheltered from wind by the Amberg massif, it is surprisingly warm for its elevation (820m/2,690ft). It even supports chestnut trees and fruit orchards. The best view of the town is from the graveyard of the hilltop Pfarrkirche (parish church) (1667–1744). Don't miss the frescoes on the Gasthof zum Stern (*see p172*). This 17th-century inn has a remarkable painted façade in which every window tells a story, either naughty or noble.
Leave Ötz on the B186, travelling south to Umhausen.

2 Stuibenfall

The base of the Stuibenfall (Stuiben Waterfall) is easily reached via a footpath from a parking area just outside Umhausen. The highest waterfall in the Tyrol, it plunges 150m (492ft) into the Ötz Valley. Like so much of the valley's geology, the waterfall was the result of falling rock – boulders sealed off the

Horlachebach River, which had to seek a new course.
Continue along the valley on the B186 to Längenfeld.

3 Längenfeld

It is only fitting that Längenfeld, the largest town in the Ötz Valley, should also have the highest church tower, which crowns Pfarrkirche St Katharina. Längenfeld is the centre of mountain climbing in the valley and the starting point for 150km (93 miles) of mountain trails. Over 150 mushers and 1,500 sleigh dogs meet here in mid-January to compete in the sleigh dog European Cup Race. The Ötztal Heimat und Freilichtmuseum (Folklore and Open-air Museum) is housed in a 300-year-old barn and mill complex.
Stay on the B186 to Sölden.

4 Sölden

As far as facilities are concerned, Sölden is exceptional. The top of the Gaislachkogel (3,040m/9,974ft) is the highest cable-car station in Austria. It is a highlight both for its downhill ski runs and the sweeping views from its panorama restaurant. A 13km (8-mile) long *Panoramastrasse* (toll road) leads from Sölden up to the glacier of the Rettenbachferner and further through the highest tunnel in Europe to the Tiefenbachferner (2,800m/9,187ft) parking area. The Venter Höhenweg starts nearby – a relatively easy 4-hour walk that tours sublime high Alpine scenery. *Stay on the B186 until it forks. Turn left into Gurgltal.*

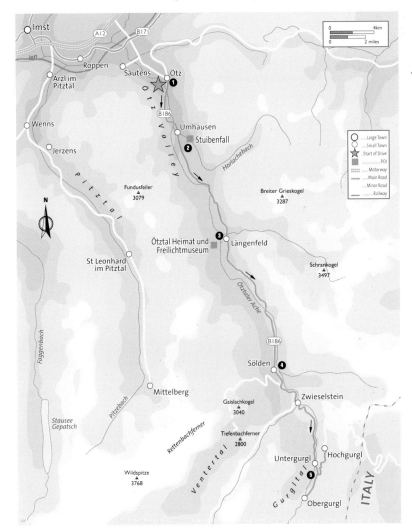

5 Gurgltal (Gurgl Valley)

There are three villages with the name 'Gurgl' (Untergurgl, Obergurgl and Hochgurgl). Together they form one of the top ski resorts in Europe that attracts older, well-heeled skiers, and is famously reliable for snow. Of the three, only Untergurgl has retained a whiff of Tyrolean village atmosphere. Obergurgl likes to call itself the highest parish in Austria (1,930m/6,332ft), and the ski resort is a starting point for memorable summer hikes to the Rotmoos Waterfall and into the stunning valley of the same name. Hochgurgl is Austria's highest ski resort (2,150m/7,054ft), with the elevation reflected in its prices. Its most prestigious ski run is an 8.5km (5¼-mile) joyride from Wurmkogel (3,082m/10,112ft) down to Untergurgl (1,280m/4,200ft).

Unless you want to go to Italy, make a U-turn and drive back to the valley.

The church in Sölden, against a glorious mountain backdrop

A typical mountainside village in the Ötz Valley

OSTTIROL

Osttirol (East Tyrol) feels like an island in the Alps rather than part of the main tourist trail. Its isolation, once a curse, has become a blessing. For now, at least, a chain of peaks and glaciers is keeping the hyperactive world from its doors. Politically, it has been a 'stepchild' since it was split from the South Tyrol. The latter was ceded to Italy by the Treaty of Versailles in 1919. The construction in 1967 of the Felbertauernstrasse (and a 5.2km/3¼-mile long tunnel) made East Tyrol accessible from the north by way of an extraordinary mountain road. Not only does the road pass through unique Alpine scenery, it also links remote valleys, each one more idyllic

than the last. This particular route forms a 'Y' by including one of the valleys, the Virgental. Depending on your choice of other valleys, the route could become an 'X' or a 'Z'.

Defereggental (Defereggen Valley)

The Defereggental is a side valley, 40km (25 miles) long, of the Isel Valley. It penetrates deep into the Bergwelt (mountain world) of East Tyrol. The main villages are Hopfgarten, once a centre for mining, St Veit and St Jakob, where the church – St Leonhard – is famous for its 15th-century frescoes and its views of the surrounding mountains. The valley harbours the largest Zirbenwald (stone-pine forest)

Lienz's valley setting

in the eastern Alps. If you want to drive to Italy, the road is an adventurous way to get there via the dizzying Staller Sattel pass (2,052m/6,732ft).

Kals am Grossglockner

Kals am Grossglockner is the principal village of the valley, lying at the foot of the Grossglockner (3,798m/12,461ft) – the 'King' of the Hohe Tauern and Austria's highest mountain (*see pp82–9*). Just outside the town, the Filialkirche St Georg comes into sight, one of the most photographed churches in the Alps. From there, the road leads up the mountain to the Kalser Glocknerstrasse, a 7km (4¹/₃-mile)

long toll road that coils its way from 1,325m (4,347ft) up to 2,000m (6,562ft), ending at a mountain lodge, the Lucknerhaus. Here, there are majestic views of the Ködnitz Valley and the summit of the Grossglockner.

Lienz

Lienz looks over its shoulder at 2,000 years of history, and wakes up every morning to awe-inspiring views of the jagged Dolomites. The only Roman city ever dug up in the Tyrol, Aguntum is in the outlying village of Dölsach, an intriguing pile of stones that was once town walls, country villas and a bathhouse. The Counts of Görz built the Italianate Schloss Bruck in the 13th century. Much of the castle is now used for a Heimatmuseum that explores the lives of peasants as well as lords. Its Romanesque chapel is graced with vivid frescoes. There is also a fine collection of work by native son Albin Egger-Lienz, a 19th-century expressionist painter who chronicled the hard life of Tyrolean farmers and miners. The Pfarrkirche St Andrä, near the castle, is one of the most important Gothic churches in the Tyrol. It is worth visiting for its harmonious interior and the exquisitely chiselled tombstones of the Counts of Görz. A 19th-century traveller wrote of Lienz: 'For many generations the city has had the custom of burning down from time to time only to be built up again'. The cycle repeated itself after four Allied bombings in 1945 and, today, the Altstadt (Old Town) has many of the same features as an American shopping mall. Blue-green Tristacher See is a lovely mountain lake just south of the town, where the water is warm enough for swimming in summer.

Matrei in Osttirol

The town of Matrei (population of 4,500) lies at an altitude of 1,000m (3,281ft), almost equidistant between the two highest peaks in Austria, the Grossglockner and the Grossvenediger. It is also the meeting point of three valleys – the Tauerntal, Virgental and Iseltal. Massive landslides destroyed

Aguntum, the excavated Roman city in Dölsach

Stunning views can be seen from the Goldriedbahn in Matrei

Matrei several times in its history. The final blow was the great fire of 1892 that damaged all but three buildings. On a clear day, the single best thing to do in Matrei is to hop on the Goldriedbahn that hoists visitors up to a mountain station (2,150m/7,054ft) for views of the Kendlspitze peak, the Virgental, the Kristallkopf and the Grossglockner. The highest and most scenic part of a famous hike – the Europa Panoramaweg – is a mere 25 minutes' walk from the station along an easy trail. The town's main artistic treasure, the St Nikolauskirche, is a short distance outside town on a hillside above the hamlet of Ganz. The Romanesque church evokes early Christianity despite the addition of Gothic elements. A naïve set of frescoes in the ground floor choir shows a chunky Adam and Eve and a clumsy fall from grace. A more refined set of frescoes in the upstairs choir, painted by an itinerant artist in Venetian-Byzantine style, reveals the four elements personified, the Apostles and the Evangelists.

Nationalpark Hohe Tauern

The Hohe Tauern National Park has an area of approximately 1,800sq km (695 sq miles) and is one of the last significant undisturbed mountain environments in the heart of Europe. It stretches over the three provinces of

Carinthia, Salzburg and Tyrol. The highest points are the Grossglockner (3,798m/12,461ft) and the Grossvenediger (3,674m/12,054ft). Geologically speaking, the Hohe Tauern is a window on time, revealing many secrets of the earth's history. The forces of upheaval and erosion have worn away layers of limestone – several kilometres thick – that were formed when the mountains were at the bottom of prehistoric seas.

What emerges is a 'profile' in stone (gneiss and schist) of the earth as it looked even earlier in time – 300 million years ago. The park is a refuge for Alpine fauna and flora.

Virgental (Virgen Valley) and Umballfälle (Umbal Falls)

The Virgental begins at Matrei where the Isel River flows between the heavily forested Lasörling ridge and the jagged peaks of the Eichham Range. Hedgerows (unusual in the eastern Alps) crisscross the valley and provide a home to creatures like the ermine. The name Virgental is from the village of Virgen, which lies on a sunny slope in the middle of the valley. The ruined castle of Rabenstein (*c*.1400) – a rectangular tower, remains of a chapel and crumbly bits of wall – occupies a narrow hilltop above it. The castle belonged to the powerful Counts of Görz. Even by feudal standards, the

Tyrol

Hohe Tauern National Park

Görz were a bad lot of rulers who ruthlessly exploited their mountain peasantry. The valley ends in a ravine encircled by 3,000m (9,800ft) peaks in their dozens and a spectacular series of waterfalls – the Umballfälle – created by the Isel, the largest glacial stream on the south side of the Hohe Tauern range. An easy 30-minute walk leads to the foot of the falls. The Wasserschaupfad Umbalfälle (Waterfalls Viewing Path) follows its course upstream with illustrations, viewpoint, benches and detailed observations about ecology, geology and water (in German). It might all seem a little pedantic, but education is crucial to the future of the falls;

ZEDLACH

Above the entrance to the Virgental Valley is Zedlach, a village of brown, weathered Tyrolean farmhouses. In winter, this is the scene of the *Klaubauf,* a kind of 'demon hunt' that dates back to pagan times. The villagers dress up in bizarre costumes and masks to chase away the spirits.

a proposed power plant, under discussion for years, would drain the water out of it.

Wallfahrtskirche Maria Schnee

The white steeple of Maria Schnee is a stunning contrast with the farmhouses of Obermauern that are almost blackened by age. It has two typical

Virgen village in Virgental

Fresco of St Christopher, Wallfahrtskirche Maria Schnee

features of pilgrimage churches in the Alps: a porch in front of the entrance so that pilgrims could wait out of the weather and, on the south side, a huge fresco of St Christopher, the patron saint of travellers. Most pilgrims in the Middle Ages could not read, and you can well imagine their excitement when they stepped through the door and caught their first glimpse of the frescoes that cover half of the nave and all of the choir. They tell the story of Christ's Passion, the life of Mary and the martyrdom of St Sebastian. Simon von Taisten, the court painter of Count Leonhard von Görz, painted them in 1484–8. He added the Earl's coat of arms on the round keystones in the choir and those of the Earl's wife, Paula von Gonzaga of Mantua. The Görz line died out shortly after the frescoes were completed with the death of Leonhard in 1500. The villagers of Virgen perform an ancient rite every Easter: they wash and comb a ram and adorn him with ribbons. The next day, they begin a procession at 6am, herding the lone ram to meet the villagers of Obermauern. A Mass in Maria Schnee follows with the ram in the central aisle. Afterwards they sacrifice it (symbolically; this is the only break with tradition). The ritual goes back to a holy vow made during a 17th-century outbreak of the plague.

Obermauern.

Bringing Alpine fauna back from extinction

The ibex, bearded vulture, marmot and lynx are among the animals that were once almost extinct but are now making a comeback in Hohe Tauern National Park. However, a surprisingly small, non-contiguous percentage of the total area of the park falls under the strictest level of protection. In other areas, skiing and hunting are still allowed. In a real sense, the battle for the park continues.

Ibex

During the Middle Ages, Austrian folk medicine regarded the *Steinbock* (ibex) as a walking pharmacy: the blood, eyes, lungs, hide and bones all had different healing properties. Princes treasured the horn of the ibex as a drinking vessel because they believed it would render poison harmless. Saint Hildegard von Bingen wrote that you should never leave the house without a dried ibex tail in your pocket, and a Salzburg archbishop, Guidobald Graf von Thun (1654–68), had a whole section of his court pharmacy devoted to ibex remedies. Unsurprisingly, given the price on its head, the last ibex was killed in the Tyrol in the early 1700s. It was

successfully reintroduced in 1953. Today, there are several herds and hundreds of ibex. In some areas, the ibex are not particularly shy because of their frequent encounters with tourists.

White-bearded vulture

Anlauf Valley is the site of a very special project: the almost extinct *Bartgeier* (white-bearded vulture, *Gypaetus barbatus*) has been bred in captivity and released back into the wild. If you are lucky, you might catch a glimpse of this rare bird of prey. The largest bird in the Alps, the white-bearded vulture is a huge scavenger with a wingspan of up to 2.6m (8½ft). It eats bones that it first smashes by dropping them from a high altitude. The ancient Egyptians worshipped the bird as the patron deity of the pharaohs.

Marmot

The cuddly *Murmeltier* (marmot) was hunted to near extinction in the 19th century for its fat. *Murmeltiersalbe* (marmot-fat lotion) is still sold in souvenir shops and is said to be just the thing for rheumatism, muscle pain, frostbite and more mysterious ailments. Marmots are now common in the Austrian Alps, and you will see the plump fellows calmly sunning themselves on the rocks and, perhaps, hear them whistling to signal one another.

Lynx

The lynx began to disappear in the 19th century in Western Europe, as forests were cleared for agriculture and its natural prey, roe deer, became scarcer. In some areas lynx began killing livestock for food, and the cat was finally hunted to extinction.

The reintroduction of the lynx in the Swiss Alps, which took place in the 1970s, is considered a success, but there is still only a small number in Austria. There is a conservation strategy in place for the lynx, approved by the Council of Europe, but its success will depend on the support of rural farming communities where the animal is still considered a threat to livestock.

The endangered white-bearded vulture

When to go

Late spring and early autumn are ideal times to visit Austria if you are not skiing. May, September and the first half of October tend to be the driest months of the year. Not only is the weather mild, there are fewer crowds and it is easy to find accommodation. In autumn, there are wine and harvest festivals all over the country. April and November are normally the wettest months.

Summer is ideal for mountaineering, thanks to the long days (light until 9pm) and snow-free trails. This is the time of year to explore the remote heights of the Hohe Tauern National Park (central Europe's largest) and to see – or climb – Austria's tallest mountain, the Grossglockner. There is, of course, always a need to be on your guard at higher elevations. Light thunderstorms are common from June to August and, above 2,000m (6,560ft), a heavy snow storm is always possible. Summer is the height of the tourist season in Salzburg and Vienna, but the opera houses are closed and you can't see the Vienna Boys' Choir or performances of the Spanish Riding School in Vienna. The roads in Salzkammergut (the lake district) are crowded, and in some towns parking is a problem.

Most tourists come to Austria in winter to ski. In a normal year, the winter snow cover lasts from December to March in the Alpine valleys and from November to May in higher regions. In most areas, snow is permanent above about 2,500m (8,200ft). There are obvious disadvantages to sightseeing at this time. Days are short, parks bare, and fountains boarded up. The museums close earlier, and some sights such as castles and caves are also closed. However, in other respects, it is an ideal time to visit Salzburg and Vienna. There are almost no tourists, and the opera and concert seasons unfold in all their glory. Both cities are charming under a layer of snow, and festive during Christmas and New Year.

Winter visitors are usually here for the skiing

Autumn can be glorious in Austria

Getting around

Vienna has 23 districts, known as Bezirke. The public transportation system, one of the best in Europe, consists of trains, trams and buses: the Schnellbahn (S-Bahn) is a fast underground train; the U-Bahn is the underground or subway; and the Strassenbahnen are trams (see map pp132–3).

By public transport

The easiest way to use the system is to purchase a *Tageskarte* (day pass) or *Wochenkarte* (week pass) that covers all public transport. There are night buses between 12.30am and 5am, when the trains stop running. It is normally possible to use the same ticket(s) for trams, buses and subways. It is often better to park your car and use public transport to explore the cities and larger towns than to drive yourself. Innsbruck, Salzburg and Vienna have combination tickets (cards) that you can buy at the tourist office (valid for 1–3 days) and use for unlimited access to the city's public transport with free or reduced admission to museums and other attractions.

By train

Austria is blessed with an extensive train system. For timetables, visit *www.oebb.at* or phone the central information line (*Tel: 05 17 17*). At most stations, you can ask for a step-by-step itinerary and have it printed out for you. Some local train stations rent bikes, allowing you to mix train and bike travel.

The *Thomas Cook European Rail Timetable*, published monthly, has details of train services and is available to buy online at

Watch your speed!

www.thomascookpublishing.com, from Thomas Cook branches in the UK or *tel: 01733 416477*.

Eurail's Austria pass is the best value for many North Americans when travelling exclusively in Austria. To travel in neighbouring countries as well, the Eurail Selectpass gives you up to 15 travel days within a two-month period in three, four or five adjacent countries. For a whirlwind tour of Europe, consider the 21-country Eurail Global pass. To check out all the options, visit *www.raileurope.com* (*Tel: 888 382 72 45*).

By car

The speed limit on the *Autobahn* is 130kph (80mph), 100kph (60mph) on B-roads (Bundesstrassen) and 50kph (30mph) in town. Speed limits are enforced and heavy on-the-spot fines can be levied. Austria has strict drink-driving laws, only allowing 0.5mg of alcohol per millilitre of blood (the UK limit is 0.8mg). Seatbelts must be worn by the driver and all passengers. Headlights must be used at all times, both night and day. A tax sticker (vignette) is required for the *Autobahn*. and you can buy one at many petrol

Trams are reliable and efficient in Austria

Getting around

stations close to the border in neighbouring countries, at car rental agencies, or in ÖAMTC (Österreichischer Automobil, Motorrad und Touring Club) offices. You will also pay a toll at the entrance of many high Alpine roads such as the Brenner Pass, Gerlospass, Felbertauernstrasse and Grossglockner Hochalpenstrasse.

By boat

Boats cruise the Danube from early April to the end of December (*Donau Schiff Wurm & Köck. www.donauschiffahrt.de*). The best way to explore many of Austria's 1,000 lakes is by boat. Ferry boats traverse the larger lakes (Achensee, Bodensee, Wolfgangsee and Attersee).

Hiring a bike is a good way to explore a city

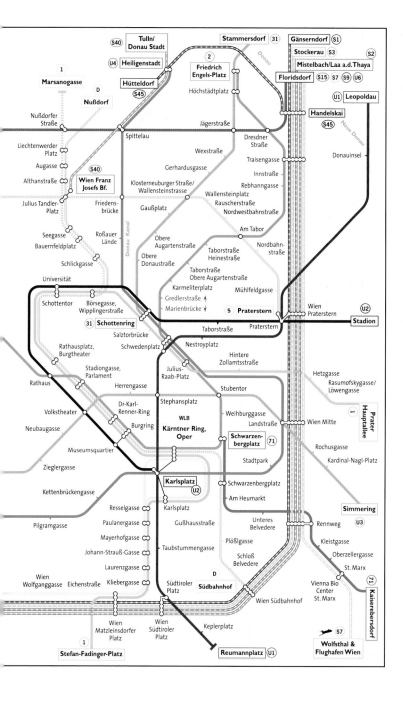

Accommodation

Austrian state authorities give ratings to hotels and pensions based on rigorous criteria and regular inspections, but they are not very useful. The classifications do not determine a hotel or pension's rates and, below the luxury level, the standards are remarkably uniform.

Hotels

Most hotel rooms are impeccably clean and comfortable, and service is usually efficient and often welcoming. Austrian hotel rates include all charges and taxes and, with rare exceptions, breakfast. Prices are frequently quoted pro person (per person, sometimes abbreviated as pp), so double-check the rate if there are two people sharing a room.

Gasthöfe

A *Gasthof* is the equivalent of an inn or pension. *Gasthöfe* are often family businesses, with the owner and family in attendance. Many have a *Gasthaus*, *Gaststätte* or *Weinstube* where you can drink local beer or wine and eat local specialities. Televisions and telephones are not standard equipment, but most *Gasthöfe* have en-suite bathrooms. Smaller pensions might not have a restaurant (but normally still serve breakfast), and the least expensive ones only have a sink in the room with shared facilities in the hall.

Private homes

Private homes and farmhouses offer the best value for money, but you might have to brave a language barrier to find them. They are registered with the local tourist offices, and staff there can usually make a reservation for you. The signs advertising the rooms will say '*Fremdenzimmer*' or '*Zimmer Frei*' (Room to Let).

Rooms are usually spotless and are likely to have a private bathroom and toilet facilities. In most places, there is a minimum stay of three nights so there may be a surcharge if you wish to spend only one night. Bed and breakfast accommodation and holiday apartments can be booked at *www.privatvermieter.at*

Farm holidays

If you are willing to book for three nights, you can take a farm holiday. This is the best way to get to know local people and their way of life. The organisation Urlaub am Bauernhof provides information (*Brixnerstrasse 1, A-6020 Innsbruck. Tel: 0592 92 11 72. Fax: 0592 92 11 79. www.urlaubambauernhof.at*).

Camping

There are campsites all over Austria. Camping without a permit is not allowed. Information is available from the Österreichischer Camping-Club (ÖCC) (*Schubertring 1–3, 1010 Wien. Tel: 711 99 27 51. Fax: 711 99 27 54. www.campingclub.at*).

ROOM RATES

Festivals, trade fairs or the peak skiing season can almost double accommodation prices and make it difficult to find a room. On the other hand, prices are often lower on the weekends in the cities and during the off- or shoulder-seasons, particularly in the Alps.

Hostels

Hostels (*Jugendherberge*) are open to all ages. Many hostels have a few double or family rooms, but you need to reserve them well in advance. *www.oejhv.or.at*

Accommodation

Hotels in Annagasse, Vienna

Food and drink

Austria is no place for a diet. The province of Tyrol claims over 300 pork dishes and sausages. Thanks to its imperial history, the country has collected all sorts of dishes from its former territories, whether it's Hungarian goulash or Schlutzkrapfen *(ravioli). Wiener Schnitzel is just one of three dozen varieties of breaded veal cutlet, and can be followed by a coffee served 40 different ways. Austria impresses with its Grüner Veltiner, Riesling and dessert wines, but it has a formidable beer culture as well.*

Food

Many Austrian hotels will serve a breakfast that keeps you going all day long: coffee or tea, fruit juices, sliced baked ham, smoked ham, liverwurst, cheeses, hard-boiled eggs, yoghurt, jams, fruit, and several kinds of bread. A *Gabelfrühstück* is a hot mid-morning snack, usually a sausage. Traditionally, lunch is the biggest meal of the day. A *Jause* is a mid-morning or mid-afternoon feast of cakes, sandwiches and coffee. The evening meal at home, by contrast, is often just a modest affair of bread and cold cuts.

One of the greatest culinary traditions of Austria is the dumpling – *Knödel*. It is made from potatoes, stale bread (*Semmelknödel*) or with liver (*Leberknödel*). The dumplings often make their way into clear broth soups such as *Markknödelsuppe*, made from bone marrow. *Spätzle* (*Nockern* in the Tyrol) are thin noodle-dumplings. *Germknödel* is a steamed dumpling smothered in a vanilla or sweet fruit

sauce. *Tafelspitz* is beef, stewed until tender and usually served with horseradish. *Hirsch* and *Wildschwein* (venison and wild boar) are eaten with great relish in autumn and winter, accompanied by wild mushrooms or in a stew. For St Martin's Day (in November) and Christmas, a goose is rubbed with herbs, carefully roasted, and served with apples and red cabbage. *Wiener Schnitzel* is a cutlet of *Kalb* (veal) or *Schwein* (pork) dredged in milk and egg, coated in breadcrumbs and sautéed. If the Tyrol has such a thing as a national dish, it is *Tiroler Gröstl* – a kind of farmer's fry-up of pork, veal and/or beef, onions, marjoram and potatoes. Portions are reminiscent of a medieval banquet. Think twice before ordering a *Tagesmenü*, which is a three-course meal (appetiser, entrée and dessert). Fish is a welcome exception to otherwise hearty cooking. You can often eat fresh trout, carp and pikeperch either *blau* (poached) or

Müllerin (lightly breaded and sautéed). Sausages are the time-honoured fast food, served in stalls, beer halls and in taverns. They come in many variations: *Weisswurst* contains veal and is eaten with sweet mustard; *Blutwurst* is made with blood; *Bratwurst* is a pork sausage that is either grilled or fried and served with a bread roll and mild mustard. Admittedly, none of this is likely to appeal to a vegetarian, but fresh, enormous salads are often on offer (mention that you want it without any *Speck* – bacon), and there are excellent mountain cheeses put to good use in dishes like *Käsespätzle* (noodles with melted cheese and caramelised onions). Bread is one of the joys of eating in Austria. Even an average corner bakery churns out a dozen varieties a day, from simple rolls to wholegrain loaves, with combinations of three or six grains.

Austria has more than its share of gourmet restaurants, which tend to combine local tradition with international culinary trends. *Neue Küche*, for example, is the Teutonic answer to nouvelle cuisine. There is a distinct difference between establishments with names like *Gaststätte*, *Bräuhaus* and *Weinstube*, and restaurants. The former serve *Gutbürgerliche Küche*, which roughly translates as 'hearty local fare'. They also function as bars or cafés where you are not necessarily expected to eat; it is fine to just order beer or coffee. In a *Gaststätte*, it is customary for strangers to share tables when no other places are available, although it is polite to ask

The café at the Festung Hohensalzburg, Salzburg

Food is a work of art in Vienna

Drinks

Coffee is the hot beverage of choice. Drinking it in a *Kaffeehaus* or *Café Konditorei* is a venerable tradition and an occasion for gossiping or reading a newspaper from the wooden rack. Coffee is available in many versions, including: ein grosser Brauner (a large espresso with a little milk or cream); *Melange* (coffee with a lot of milk) and *ein kleiner Mokka* (a very small, concentrated espresso). Coffee often goes well with a dessert or rich pastry, such as strudel or the decadent chocolate cake called *Sachertorte.*

Tea is generally served as a cup of hot water with a tea bag on the side. Tap water (*Leitungswasser*) is perfectly safe to drink everywhere, and the tap water in Vienna is actually piped from the mountains, but some Austrians prefer bottled water.

Drinking beer is a major pastime in Austria. The spring *Gauderfest* (*see p113*) in the Tyrol pays homage to beer in the same way as the more famous *Octoberfest*. Pilsner is the most popular beer but there are many others, of various shades (*Hell* means 'amber'; *Dunkel* means 'deep brown') and strengths – beware any beer with the suffix '-ator'. *Weizenbier* or *Weissbier* (wheat beer) is especially popular in summer; it is often served with a slice of lemon. A *Radler* is a refreshing mix of beer and lemonade.

Austria's most important wine regions are Burgenland, the Wachau and Styria. White wines greatly

first. Foreigners often inadvertently break a taboo by sitting down at a table marked 'Stammtisch'. The *Stammtisch* is for regulars and strictly off limits to anyone else. Cafés fall into two categories: trendy places with ultramodern décor, or the elegant, pre-war *Kaffeehaus* where Austrians ritually consume *Kaffee und Kuchen* (coffee and cake). Some butcher shops and bakeries have a *Steh-café* (Standing Café) with high tables for eating a snack standing up. An *Imbiss* is another place for a quick snack, either standing up or sitting in a plastic chair.

outnumber reds, reflecting Austria's northern climate. The cheaper Austrian wines are labelled as *Tafelwein* and *Landwein*. *Qualitätswein* is the next step up, followed by *Prädikatswein* and *Qualitätswein Kabinett*. The classifications *Spätlese* and *Auslese* mean the grapes were harvested late in the year, resulting in a naturally sweet wine full of distinctive flavours. Traditional restaurants in wine regions usually serve *Offene Weine* (wines by the glass and carafe) from the region. People eating together are not necessarily expected to share a carafe of the same wine. They can order separately, by the 'glass', either an *achtel* (0.125 litres/$^{1}/_{4}$ pint) or a *viertele* (almost 0.25 litres/$^{1}/_{2}$ pint served in a large glass or mini-carafe). Autumn is the season for drinking young, freshly fermenting wine (*Sturm*), and summer is the time for a *Schörle*, wine mixed with mineral water or soda.

Kaffee und Kuchen

Entertainment

There is more to entertainment in Austria than symphonic music and ballroom dancing. If you do want to waltz, the season in Vienna runs from December to March. But Vienna's club scene is hot, and there are plenty of late-night or all-night bars in the first district. Salzburg and Innsbruck also have a surprising number of bars, clubs and discos. The major ski resorts pulse with a mind-boggling spectrum of nightlife, from disco to folklore.

Vienna

The Staatsoper and the Volksoper opera houses perform daily in Vienna, except during July and August (*see pp38 & 42*). The Vienna Boys' Choir can be heard in several locations (*see their website www.wsk.at for details*). Cheaper standing room tickets are often available shortly before performances begin. Once inside, you can tie a sweater or scarf to the rails or balcony

Lipizzaner stallions from the Spanish Riding School in Vienna

to 'reserve' your place while you go to the bar. The Spanish Riding School has Sunday performances in Vienna (*early Mar–end June; Sept–end Oct*) (*see p31*).

The coffee houses of Vienna and Salzburg are still the scene for animated discussions, much as they were in the days when frequented by Trotsky and Freud. Another Vienna tradition – the balls – is also alive and well. From 31 December until Ash Wednesday, Vienna becomes one big ballroom. There are balls for everybody, from the famous Opera Ball to the Ball of Bad Taste. You can also take crash courses to brush up on your waltzing steps.

The so-called Bermuda Triangle (Bermuda Dreieck) (*just south of the Danube Canal near St Ruprecht's church*) is packed with bars and clubs, some of them staging live music. Most of the bars stay open until 4am or later, and all night on weekends. The Volksgarten, situated in the palace gardens, is several venues in one, with a garden bar and a dance floor that suddenly becomes open to the elements when the roof parts.

Salzburg

Salzburg, the birthplace of Mozart, has music festivals almost monthly, culminating in a five-week-long artistic banquet of opera, theatre, church choirs, folk music, classical concerts and Austrian marionette theatre performances (*from late July & through Aug*). One of the best ways to experience the Hohensalzburg Fortress in Salzburg is to attend one of the almost nightly chamber music concerts (*www.mozartfestival.at*). These are held in the Golden Hall, or Prince's Chamber, a wood-panelled stateroom built in about 1500. Although it's more famous for Mozartmania, Salzburg has a serious jazz and rock scene. Concerts, theatre performances, music festivals and other events are listed at the pages of *www.salzburginfo.at*

Volkstheater, Vienna

Innsbruck

In Innsbruck, Ambras castle hosts classical music concerts in summer, and a medieval brass band performs from the city's Golden Roof balcony. 'Tyrolean evenings' feature folk dancing, yodelling and brass bands. There are year-round performances of opera and ballet at the Landestheater.

Après-ski

After a long hard day on the slopes, skiers from across the globe fill up the venues in Austria's myriad ski resorts, many of which become cosmopolitan villages for a couple of months each year. You will find clubs, bars and eateries of almost every description in places like Mayrhofen and Kitzbühel. There are places with oompah-sing-along songs where the Germanophones are more likely to congregate, live country blues, techno and even the odd traditional English pub.

Casinos

There's no admission charge to enter casinos but you have to show identification. While no one will mistake it for Las Vegas, Vienna is home to two of Europe's biggest poker rooms, the Concord Card Casino and Poker World. For something more traditional, take the train to the spa town of Baden-bei-Wien. The Baden Casino (*www.casinos.at*) is a restored palace with ornate décor, frescoed ceilings, garden fountains and an excellent restaurant.

Shopping

Shopping is a popular pastime in Austria. On the pedestrian Kärntner Strasse in Vienna, even sub-zero temperatures can't keep Viennese locals from taking strolls or from window-shopping at the various department stores or boutiques.

Popular Austrian souvenirs include petit-point needlework, knitwear, loden-cloth coats and jackets, Tyrolean hats, *Dirndls* (dresses), down quilts, hand-painted porcelain, wood carvings and dolls, woollens, leather goods and crystal. Art lovers will find a treasure trove in antique shops and at frequently held auctions. The Vienna auction house, the Dorotheum, is the largest in central Europe.

The outdoor markets offer local colour as well as handicrafts and the makings of a picnic. Visit flea markets on Saturdays to find some unusual gifts. Advent or Christmas markets have a long tradition in Austria, and can be found in most cities. Other items to consider are: *Bergkäse* (mountain cheese); *Kerzen* (candles); *Schnitzfiguren* (carved wooden figures, usually religious in theme); *Obstbrand* also called *Schnaps*; *Kristallglas* (crystal); *Schinkenspeck* (smoked ham); and jewellery from *Halbedelsteinen* (semi-precious stones).

Trachten (folk costumes) are never sold in souvenir shops. The items sold there are cheap copies made in China or Korea. If you want a real Tyrolean hat, *Schultertuch* (shawl), *Dirndl* (dress) or *Lederhosen* (leather trousers), go to a local tailor or dressmaker.

Austria has Value Added Tax (VAT) added to most goods and services. In theory, visitors from outside the EU are entitled to a refund of this tax on purchases exceeding 75 euros from any one store. In practice, it is time-consuming to obtain the refund. Look for the 'Tax-Free Shopping' sign in the shop window and ask the clerk for the necessary paperwork. The papers must be stamped by a customs official before or upon leaving Austria. You then proceed to the tax-free cashpoint at the airport or border station to receive most of your tax back as a refund. You will not receive a refund without the proper, stamped paperwork. You may be asked to show the goods you are exporting under this exemption.

The Christmas Market in Vienna

Sport and leisure

Austria is one of the most sports-minded countries in the world. Thanks to its Alpine geography, there are places where you can ski, golf and swim all on the same day. Local guides and companies offer you the opportunity to climb or jump off mountains, run the countless white-water rivers or fly like a bird.

Airborne

Airborne sports range from sailplaning and paragliding to hot-air ballooning. Austria has some of the best Alpine ballooning in Europe, over the Alpine ranges of the Salzkammergut and the steppe-like landscape around Neusiedl Lake. The facilities for paragliding are top class. If wind conditions are right, an experienced paraglider can hop from peak to peak.

Cycling

Cycling is very popular along the Inn and the Danube rivers. There are also spectacular routes for mountain bikers on designated trails in Hohe Tauern National Park and in the Tyrolean Alps.

Golf

Many of Austria's 150 golf courses were built in the last 15 years. Zell am See Golf Club is at the foot of the 3,000m (9,843ft) Kitzsteinhorn Mountain. The Mondsee Golf Club is wrapped around the lake of the same name at the foot of the Drachenwand. Gold Egg is an 18-hole course that zigzags around working dairy farms.

Mountain climbing and hiking

Austria lends itself to walking and climbing as well as skiing. Extended hikes often involve staying overnight in

A cable car will get you to the start of your hike

There's plenty to look at as you ski down

mountain huts. There are thousands of kilometres of hiking and mountain routes carefully signposted and cross-referenced to detailed maps. In the Tyrol, paths are colour-coded using the same system as for skiing: blue for easy; red for moderate; and black where some climbing might be necessary.

Often, the best way to start a hike is to take a cable car first. The mountains pose many hazards, including sunburn (particularly on snow), altitude sickness (the first symptoms are headaches, nausea and dizziness), and hypothermia (a fall in the body's internal temperature). Ticks can be a problem in some lower-elevation forests. If you find one buried in your skin, do not pull it out; instead, coat it with oil or salt and it should dislodge itself. Alpine streams look pristine but are not always safe to drink from. Boil the water for ten minutes before drinking it, or use iodine tablets like Potable Aqua.

Skiing

Austria is a paradise for skiers, with spectacular scenery and everything from nursery slopes to the most challenging ski runs. There is even year-round skiing on some glaciers at the higher elevations such as Stubai in the Tyrol. It pays to shop around for your holiday since lesser-known resorts can cost half as much as internationally

There are a few places where you can go whitewater rafting

Mountaineering
Österreichischer Alpenverein
(Austrian Alpine Club).
www.bergsteigen.at

Hiking
www.wanderdoerfer.at

Skiing
www.europasportregion.info

Water sports
Alpinschule Club Monté, Salzburg.
www.montee.com
Oesterreichischer Kanuverband.
www.kanuverband.at
Osttirol Adventures (canyoning
and kayaking).
www.osttirol-adventures.at

Fishing
www.fischwasser.com

Cycling
www.radtouren.at

Golf
Gold Egg. *www.seehof-goldegg.com*
Mondsee Golf Club. *www.golfclubmondsee.at*
Österreichischer Golf-Verband
(Austrian Golf Club). *www.golf.at*
Zell am See Golf Club at Kaprun.
www.europasportregion.at/golfclub

Ballooning and Paragliding
ÖAEC, Österreichischer Aero-Club
(Austrian Aero Club).
www.aeroclub.at

Paragliding in Zillertal

known, popular ones. Other winter
activities include horse-drawn
sleigh rides, natural ice skating
and local curling.

Water sports

Water sports include swimming, skin
diving, sailing, surfing, waterskiing
and boating.

Most of the rivers and lakes are clean
enough to swim in, and you can swim
for free in some places, but many of the
lakeside beaches have an entrance fee.
You can hire paddle boats in lakeside
resorts as well as rowing boats and
motorboats. Rafting takes the form of
shooting the mountain rapids in the
Alps, notably on the Isel and Drau in
Osttirol (East Tyrol) and the Lammer
and Salzach in Salzburg province.
Fishing permits are best arranged
through the local tourist office.

Country of spas

There are health resorts extending from Bad Hall in Upper Austria, across the Salzkammergut and the magnificent valley of the Gasteiner Ache, to Solebad Hall-in-Tyrol. The resorts draw people from all over the world in search of health and well-being. You can combine spa breaks with golf, hiking, skiing and sightseeing. Or wine tasting – Baden-bei-Wien, in the Vienna Woods, is surrounded by 100 vineyards and dozens of Heurigen (wine taverns).

Chalybeate waters, radioactive springs, mineral-saline waters, sulphur

The Felsentherme spa at Bad Gastein

springs containing iodine or bromide, and mineral waters of the most varying kinds are fed into Finnish saunas, *Dampfbaden* (steam baths) and hot pools. They are used therapeutically for drinking or bathing cures, inhalations or medicinal packs. Tyrol's Bad Häring health and rehabilitation centre offers Austria's first Cold Chamber with temperatures of 120°C below zero (−184°F). This so-called cryotherapy is used to alleviate pain and enhance performance.

There is a whole host of esoteric treatments available, from sea-salt peels, lymphatic drainage and the floatarium to a saltwater pool with piped-in ambient music. Bad Eisenkappel, a health spa in the southwestern Austrian province of Carinthia, offers a relaxing soak in a bubbly brown bath of melted chocolate (the cocoa butter protects the skin from wrinkling).

Baden-bei-Wien lies among forested hills and extensive vineyards in the Vienna Woods, Wienerwald, and its sulphur springs were valued by the Romans. The town's villas, manicured park and promenades were a favourite resort for statesmen, artists and the fashionable Habsburg Empire. Bad Gastein, situated amid the impressive panorama of the Salzberg Tauern, has become Austria's most famous medicinal spa with a varied profusion of pump rooms, villas and modern hotel spas that tower above and around the natural amphitheatre created by the rushing, foaming, cascading Gasteiner Ache. Mountain sun and the purity of the air add to the effect of the radioactive thermal waters.

Some of Austria's spas have special offers for children and even babies. Sonnentherme Lutzmannsburg (*www.sonnentherme.com*) claims to have Europe's longest water slide. It also has a 'baby world' and a children's steam room. The Therme Oberlaa (*www.oberlaa.at*), located in the middle of Vienna, is also child-friendly, with purified kiddy pools and poolside babysitting.

Burgenland
www.thermenwelt.at

Gastein Valley
www.badgastein.at
www.badhofgastein.at
www.hoteldorf.com

Lower Austria
www.baden-bei-wien.at/english.htm

Salzkammergut
www.thermenhotel-badischl.at

Styria
www.thermenland.at

Tyrol
www.aquadome.at

Children

From boat rides on the Danube to dancing white horses, the Vienna Boys' Choir and legendary chocolate cake, Austria has much to inspire a child's imagination. In practical terms, it offers all sorts of child-friendly facilities such as hotels with baby monitors and ski schools for young 'snowflakes'.

Accommodation

Most hotels and pensions readily accommodate families. There is also an association of family-friendly hotels (*Kinderhotels*). Most of the hotels are located in the countryside (there is one in Vienna). Some have swimming pools and spas, others have winter ski schools, and several are located on farms. All of them have facilities and activities tailored to parents and their little ones, including childcare, toys and essential baby stuff. Not all of the hotels have activities in English, so call ahead to find out.
www.babyhotel.at
www.kinderhotels.co.uk

Eating out

Children are generally welcome in pubs and cafés as long as adults accompany them, but they are rarely smoke-free. High chairs are widely available.

Transport

In Austria, children under the age of 13 are required by law to sit in the back seat of a vehicle if it has one. Safety seats for children under four are strongly recommended, although not required by law. If you hire a car, consider bringing child seats with you; rental car companies impose an extra daily charge per safety seat.

In Vienna, children under 15 ride for free on the underground, trams and buses during school holidays and all Sundays and public holidays. At other

Explore the waterfront at Gmunden

Play I-spy from Salzburg's castle

times, you can buy discounted tickets at tobacconists or vending machines.

What to do

Austria is full of castles, museums and zoos that appeal to children. There are cable cars, steam trains and ferry boats to ride on. Many ski resorts are geared to family ski holidays, with a school for 'snowflakes' (confirm that they have instruction in English) and babysitting options to entertain the children while you ski. Among Vienna's hundred museums, many will interest children. Apart from the fairground (*www.prater.at*), there are attractions such as the Minopolis (*www.minopolis.at*) and Butterfly House (*www.schmetterlinghaus.at*) that are sometimes overlooked. In Innsbruck, the Alpenzoo (Alpine Zoo, *see p104*) and the armoury at Schloss Ambras (*see p107*) are just two of the possible highlights of a kid's holiday. Salzburg's marionettes at the Marionettentheater are the perfect introduction to opera for children and they will revel in the trick fountains of Schloss Hellbrunn (*see p72*). Easy mountain hikes, salt mines (Hallstatt, *see p100*) and ice caves (Dachstein, *see p95*) are a fun and memorable way to teach children about geography.

Essentials

Arriving
By air
There are daily flights from London to Austria. Generally, the earlier you book, the cheaper the tickets. There is a train every half an hour between Vienna Schwechat airport and Vienna's central train station (district 3); travel time is 16 minutes. The Franz-Josef-Flughafen airport in Munich is much closer to Salzburg and the Tyrol (only 90 minutes by car).

From the UK
British Airways and Lufthansa have flights several times a day and there are many fly/drive packages on offer from London, Manchester and Birmingham. Online sources of information for last-minute flights include *www.cheapflights.co.uk*; *www.lastminute.com*; and *www.flightline.co.uk*

The advantages of bringing your own car are obvious, but travelling to Austria from the UK Channel ports means spending two days on the *Autobahn*, there and back. London, as the European capital of discount flights, offers many alternatives.

From the US and Canada
Germany is one of the cheaper transatlantic destinations, particularly Frankfurt and, to a lesser extent, Munich. American Airlines, United Airlines and Air Canada all have regularly scheduled flights.

AIRLINES

Air Berlin Tel: 0871 5000 737 (UK), 1 866 266 5588 (US & Canada), +49 01805 737800 (Germany). *www.ltu.com*
Austrian Airlines Tel: 0870 124 2625 (UK), 1 800 843 0002 (US). *www.aua.com*
BA Tel: 0844 493 0787. *www.ba.com*
easyJet Tel: 0905 560 7777. *www.easyjet.com*
Flybe Tel: 0871 700 2000. *www.flybe.com*
Jet2 Tel: 0871 226 1737. *www.jet2.com*
Lufthansa Tel: 0871 945 9747 (UK), 1 800 399 5838 (US). *www.lufthansa.com*
Ryanair Tel: 0871 246 0000. *www.ryanair.com*
Thomsonfly Tel: 0870 190 0737. *www.thomsonfly.com*
United Airlines Tel: 1 800 864 8331 (US), 1 800 538 2929 (International). *www.united.com*

Search for low fares and fly-drive
www.travelocity.com
www.expedia.com
www.cheaptickets.com

Customs
An EU citizen can take generous quantities of everything for personal use into Austria (within reason; a truckload of whisky invites a few questions). Non-EU citizens must content themselves with: 200 cigarettes, 50 cigars, 1 litre of spirits (over 22 per cent proof) or 2 litres of wine, 0.5kg coffee, 50g of perfume or 0.25 litres of eau de cologne.

Electricity

The supply in Austria is 220 volts. Plugs are of the European type with two round prongs. All UK appliances will work with an adaptor. American appliances need a transformer.

Money

An ATM (cash machine) debit card and, as a backup, a credit card are indispensable. You can safely count on paying with plastic at petrol stations, chain hotels, expensive restaurants and touristy shops. However, to the amazement and potential embarrassment of many foreign tourists, a lot of other places do not accept anything but cash.

Opening hours

Opening hours, set by a combination of law and tradition, are utterly confusing in Austria. Larger shops in Austria open early and close at 8pm on weekdays and 5pm on Saturday; they are closed on Sunday. Smaller shops in Austria close at 6pm on weekdays and for lunch as well; they are open on Saturday until 1pm and closed on Sunday (some shops might open on Saturday afternoon as well). Outside regular shopping hours, the train stations of big cities are open and sell groceries. Banks are open Monday to Wednesday and Friday 8am–12.30pm and 1.30–3pm; on Thursday they are open 8am–12.30pm and 1.30–5.30pm (head offices do not close for lunch). Tourist offices are open 9am–6pm on weekdays and until 1pm

on Saturdays (in touristy places, they keep longer hours). Petrol stations on the *Autobahn* are open 24 hours a day. Restaurants will normally open at 11am and close around 11pm; many of them close in the afternoon. Traditional inns are more likely to serve food in the afternoon (*durchgehend* means 'open throughout the day') or late at night.

Passports and visas

Citizens of the EU, US, Australia, Canada and New Zealand do not require a visa, only an official identity card (a passport is the norm) to enter Austria. Non-EU citizens need a passport (valid for at least three months from the date of entry).

Post

Post offices are normally open Monday–Friday 8am–6pm and Saturday 8am/9am–noon. They have many services, so make sure you go to the right counter for *Briefmarken* (stamps) and *Pakete* (parcels). You can also change money at a post office.

Town clock, Salzburg

Essentials

The larger post offices have public fax-phones that accept a phonecard.

Suggested reading and media
Books
Autumn Sonata: Selected Poems of Georg Trakl translated by Daniel Simko
A Nervous Splendour and *Thunder at Twilight* by Frederic Morton
The Habsburg Monarchy 1809–1918 by A J P Taylor
Libelei (Playing with Love) by Arthur Schnitzler
Der Mann ohne Eigenschaften (The Man without Qualities) by Robert von Musil

Mozart and the Wolf Gang by Anthony Burgess
Schachnovelle (Chess Novella) and *Sternstunden der Menscheit (The Tide of Fortune)* by Stefan Zweig
Summer at Gaglow by Esther Freud

Films
Amadeus (1984)
The Sound of Music (1965)
The Third Man (1949)

Telephones
Public telephones in Austria use phonecards – buy them at tobacco shops or post offices. You can use

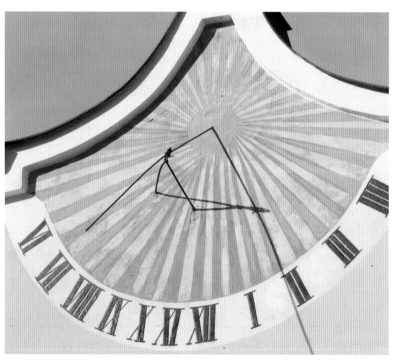

Sundial, Schloss Hellbrunn

prepaid international phonecards on public phones as well as hotel phones (otherwise, hotels are pricey for international calls). Austria has an excellent mobile telephone network. It is, of course, advisable to confirm the best mobile option before leaving home. American mobile phones will work if they are GSM-enabled. When speaking long distance, you omit the 0 from the area code. The international code for Austria is *43*.

Time

Austria is GMT + 1 hour. The difference is increased to 2 hours during 'daylight savings'. This begins at the end of March, when clocks are set ahead an hour, and ends in the autumn when they are set back an hour.

Toilets

In public toilets you are expected to pay 50 euro cents to an attendant to use the facilities (*Herren* for men and *Damen* for women). Outside the tourist zones, it is usually acceptable to enter a café to use the toilet.

Tourist information

Austria has tourist offices in almost every town and in many villages. They are located at or near the main railway station and/or on the market square. They usually have city maps that show where parking is available. They can help with finding a room (sometimes charging a small fee), and are particularly useful for

accommodation at smaller pensions or private homes.

Travellers with disabilities

Many museums, theatres, cinemas and public buildings have access ramps for wheelchairs and, increasingly, trams are being equipped to handle wheelchairs. Tourist offices will readily help travellers with disabilities find a hotel, public toilet, etc. Major hotel chains normally offer special facilities. Parking is free for people with disabilities in the blue zones of cities and towns if you have an international disabled sticker for the car.

Useful websites

Austria
www.austria-aktiv.at
www.austria.info
www.niederoesterreich.at
www.oberoesterreich.at
www.tiscover.at
www.tiscover.com
Burgenland
www.burgenland.at
Salzburg
www.salzburgerland.com
www.salzburginfo.at
Salzkammergut
www.salzkammergut.at
Tyrol
www.tirol.at
Vienna
www.wien-tourismus.at
Wachau
www.wachau.at

Language

English is widely spoken in Austria. Most of the hotels, restaurants and sports stores that rent or sell sporting equipment will have English-speaking staff. Here are a few useful words and phrases to give you a headstart.

DIRECTIONS		SIGNS	
Where is...?	Wo ist...?	one-way street	Einbahnstrasse
How do I get to...?	Wie erreicht man...?	get into lane, merge	einordnen
How far is it from here?	Wie weit ist es?	road works	Baustelle
street	die Strasse	campsite	Campingplatz
lane	Gasse	danger	Gefahr
town	die Stadt	open	geöffnet
village	das Dorf	closed	geschlossen
suburb	der Vorort	no entry	Eingang verboten
neighbourhood	Stadtteil	emergency exit	Notausgang
north	Nord	entrance	Eingang
south	Süd	exit	Ausgang
east	Ost	toilet	Toilette
west	West	Ladies/Gents	Damen/Herren
behind	hinter	push/pull	drücken/ziehen
in front of	vor	bank	Bank
opposite	gegenüber	bureau de change	Wechselstube
straight ahead	geradeaus	police	Polizei
left	links	hospital	Krankenhaus
right	rechts	pharmacy	Apotheke
at the traffic light	an der Ampel	post office	Post
at the next corner	an der nächste Ecke	airport	Flughafen
		customs	Zoll
		railway station	Bahnhof
		occupied	besetzt
		pedestrian zone	Fussgängerzone
		picnic area	Rastplatz

DRIVING

car hire	Autovermietung
petrol station	Tankstelle
petrol	Benzin
unleaded	bleifrei
my car has broken down	mein Auto hat eine Panne
accident	Autounfall
garage (for auto repair)	Autowerkstatt
parking place	Parkplatz
no parking	Parking verboten
driver's licence	Führerschein
insurance	Versicherung
junction, intersection	Kreuzung
ferry	Fähre

DAYS AND MONTHS

Monday	Montag
Tuesday	Dienstag
Wednesday	Mittwoch
Thursday	Donnerstag
Friday	Freitag
Saturday	Samstag
Sunday	Sonntag

January	Januar
February	Februar
March	März
April	April
May	Mai
June	Juni
July	Juli
August	August
September	September
October	Oktober
November	November
December	Dezember

NUMBERS

one	eins
two	zwei
three	drei
four	vier
five	fünf
six	sechs
seven	sieben
eight	acht
nine	neun
ten	zehn
eleven	elf
twelve	zwölf
thirteen	dreizehn
fourteen	vierzehn
fifteen	fünfzehn
sixteen	sechszehn
seventeen	siebzehn
eighteen	achtzehn
nineteen	neunzehn
twenty	zwanzig
twenty-one	einundzwanzig
thirty	dreissig
thirty-one	einunddreissig
forty	vierzig
fifty	fünfzig
sixty	sechszig
seventy	siebzig
eighty	achtzig
ninety	neunzig
one hundred	hundert
two hundred	zweihundert
one thousand	tausend
three thousand	dreitausend
one hundred thousand	hunderttausend
one million	eine Million

Emergencies

Accidents

If you have a serious accident in Austria, you are required by law to wait for the police to arrive. Emergency services are highly efficient and will arrive quickly, by helicopter if need be.

Car breakdowns

The first thing to do if you have a breakdown is to pull off the road, if possible. Then place a warning triangle 100m (328ft) behind the vehicle. If you are on an *Autobahn*, look for an emergency telephone (located at 2km/1¼ mile intervals), lift the phone and wait for a dispatcher to respond. You can also phone *120* directly for emergency assistance (*see below*). You will have to pay for towing and parts. However, if you are a member of an automobile club in your own country, you should be able to arrange for reciprocal coverage in Austria.

EMERGENCY TELEPHONE NUMBERS

Emergency services (*Rettungsdienst*): *144*
Ambulance (*Ärztenotdienst*): *141*
Fire (*Feuerwehr*): *122*
Police (*Polizei*): *133*
Information on snow conditions: *www.lawine.at*
Mountain emergencies (*Bergrettung*): *140*
Austrian auto club, ÖAMTC (Österreichischer Automobil, Motorrad und Touring Club): *120*
Austrian motoring association ARBÖ (Auto, Motor und Radfahrerbund Österreichs): *123*

Crime

Austria does not have a serious crime problem, and Vienna is one of the safer European capitals. Common sense will go a long way – lock the car, steer clear of dubious neighbourhoods and hold on to a wallet, camera or handbag. It is best to wear handbags across the body and keep wallets in a belt purse. If a robbery or break-in does occur, report it immediately to the police. You will need a report number for an insurance claim. By law, a person is always required to carry identification such as a passport.

Insurance

No one should leave their home country without travel insurance. However, citizens of EU countries are entitled to free emergency medical care in a public hospital. To benefit from this, EU nationals and non-EU nationals residing in the EU should carry a European Health Insurance Card (EHIC) available online at *www.ehic.org.uk*, by calling *0845 606 2030* or from post offices. Everyone else needs travel or private medical insurance.

Car drivers should have collision damage waiver insurance (American Express and some other credit card companies cover this if you rent a car with their card and turn down, in writing, the rental car's insurance policy). Car drivers will also need

Take care on switchback mountain roads

personal accident insurance for medical costs (this is included in travel insurance); and they will need liability insurance, which protects against legal claims (most rental car agencies charge extra for this).

Pharmacy

The German word for pharmacy or chemist is *Apotheke*. Your nearest pharmacy may not always be open when you need it, but a nearby pharmacy will be – they take turns in staying open for emergencies. The address and telephone number of the nearest open pharmacy is posted on the door of all the other *Apotheken*. Once you get to the one that is 'open', you still have to ring the doorbell to be served.

Directory

Accommodation price guide

Prices of accommodation are based on an average double room for two people sharing, including breakfast.

★	up to €50
★★	€51–125
★★★	€126–200
★★★★	over €200

Eating out price guide

In the restaurant listings, the star ratings indicate the average cost per person for a three-course meal, excluding alcohol. Most of the restaurants and taverns mentioned in this book serve local cuisine. The service charge is included in the bill, and tipping is not required but it is common to 'round up' the amount of the bill – pay €40 for a €38 bill, for example. Do not tip with a credit card.

★	up to €15
★★	€16–30
★★★	€31–50
★★★★	over €50

VIENNA

ACCOMMODATION

Wombat's City Hostel ★
Impeccably clean with a bar, terrace and garden, this hostel has been awarded the Austrian Eco-Label.
Grangasse 6.
Tel: 897 23 36.
www.wombats.at

Hotel Zipser ★★
Family-run hotel just behind the Rathaus.
Lange Gasse 49.
Tel: 404 54 0.
www.zipser.at

Pension Altstadt ★★
This is not your ordinary B&B; it is stylish, with individually decorated rooms and a plushy velvet salon.
Kirchengasse 41.
Tel: 522 66 66.
www.altstadt.at

Pension Nossek ★★
Lots of 19th-century style and 20th-century mod cons in this third-floor B&B.
Graben 17.
Tel: 533 70 410.
www.pension-nossek.at

Das Triest ★★★★
Designer Terence Conran has converted this former coach house into a high-tech boutique hotel.
Wiedner Haupstrasse 12.
Tel: 589 18 0.
www.dastriest.at

Hotel Imperial ★★★★
This palatial hotel is used by visiting heads of state. It is located near the Musikverein hall.
Kärntner Ring 16.
Tel: 501 10 0.
www.starwoodhotels.at

EATING OUT

Café Griensteidl ★
A classic Viennese coffee house facing the Hofburg, where tourists mingle with opera-lovers and civil servants.
Michaelisplatz 2.
Tel: 535 26 92 0.

Café Prückel ★
Coffee cups from another era (*c.*1900) and

contemporary poetry readings taking place in the back room.
Stubenring 24.
Tel: 512 61 15.

Café Sperl ★
One of the only cafés left with an original *Jugendstil* interior.
Gumpendofer Strasse 11.
Tel: 586 41 58.
www.cafesperl.at

Centimeter ★
Wurst sliced by the centimetre (or metre). Beer is served by the glass – or by the keg.
Stiftsgasse 4. Tel: 524 33 29.
www.centimeter.at

Glacisbeisl ★
Traditional Austrian cooking in the Museum Quarter.
Breite Gasse 4.
Tel: 526 56 60.

Gulaschmuseum ★
Fifteen kinds of Hungarian goulash.
Schulerstrasse. 20.
Tel: 512 10 17.
www.gulasch.at

Museum Café ★
The 1899 original interior was designed by the father of minimalism, architect Adolf Loos.
Friedrichstrasse 6.
Tel: 586 52 02.

Sirbu ★
One of the best *Heurige* (wine taverns), with great views of Vienna.
Kahlenberger Strasse 210.
Tel: 320 59 28. Open: mid-Apr–mid-Oct. Bus: 38A Armbrustergasse, then a short walk or taxi.

Café Central ★★
An institution in the traditional coffee house landscape, having opened in 1860. The Russian Bolshevik exile Trotsky, under his real name Bronstein, spent his days talking and playing chess here.
Herrengasse 14. Tel: 533 37 64 26.

Café Diglas ★★
Art Deco ambience and plenty of coffee house *kultur*. The food is as good as the coffee, and there are some vegetarian dishes.
Wollzeile 10. Tel: 512 57 65. www.diglas.at

Café Jelinek ★★
Tiny and intimate with great homemade cake and regular art exhibits.
Otto Bauergasse 5.
Tel: 597 41 13.

Lusthaus ★★
The Emperor's former hunting pavilion is a suitably elegant setting for a memorable summer's evening.
Freudenau 254.
Tel: 728 95 65.
www.lusthaus-wien.at

Meixner Gastwirtschaft ★★
This is an *edelbeisl*, a gourmet version of a traditional Viennese eatery. It also serves some Mediterranean dishes.
Buchengasse 64.
Tel: 604 27 10.

Plachutta ★★
The speciality of the house is *Tafelspitz* – a classic Austrian dish of beef stewed until it is perfectly tender and served with horseradish.
Wollzeile 38.
Tel: 512 15 77 0.

Wrenkh ★★
Vienna's best vegetarian restaurant.
Bauernmarkt 10.
Tel: 533 15 26.
www.wrenkh.at

Café Landtmann ★★★
Sigmund Freud's favourite café. It fills up with actors from the Burgtheater next door. Piano music is played from 4–7pm. In summer, chairs are put out on the Ringstrasse.

Dr Karl-Lueger-Ring 4.
Tel: 241 00 0.
www.landtmann.at

Mraz und Sohn ★★★
Chef Markus Mraz and
his sons Manuel and
Lukas are devoted to
doing new things with
traditional Austrian
cooking. Be prepared for
culinary revelations.
Wallensteinstrasse 59.
Tel: 330 45 94.
www.mraz-sohn.at. Open:
Mon–Fri 11am–3pm &
6.30pm–midnight.

**Zu Den Drei
Husaren ★★★★**
The 'Three Hussars'
serves gourmet
versions of traditional
Austrian fare.
Weihburggasse 4.
Tel: 512 10 92 0.
www.drei-husaren.at

ENTERTAINMENT
You can buy tickets for
the Staatsoper and
Volksoper in advance by
mail or at the box office
of the Bundestheater
(Operngasse 2.
Tel: 514 44 0) or at
www.bundestheater.at.
Tickets can be ordered
with a credit card by
calling 513 15 13. The
Vienna Ticket Service

(Boersegasse 1. Tel: 534 17
0) is a good service for
musicals and festivals.

If calling from abroad,
don't forget to add the
international code (43)
for Austria and the city
code (1) for Vienna.

B72
DJs and live bands.
Hernalser Gürtel/
Stadtbahnbogen 72.
Tel: 409 21 28.
www.b72.at.
Open: 8pm–4am. U-Bahn
Alser Strasse; tram 43.

Birdland
An intimate jazz club
in the Hilton Vienna run
by jazz keyboardist Joe
Lawinul. Attracts local
and global talent.
Am Stadtpark 3
(entrance via Landstrasser
Hauptstrasse 2).
www.birdland.at. Open:
7pm–2am. Closed: Mon.

Flex
One of the top DJ clubs
in Europe, with a
legendary sound system.
Located at the corner of
Danube canal and
Augarten Bridge.
Tel: 533 75 25.
www.flex.at. U-Bahn:
Schottenring.

Jazzland
Vienna's oldest jazz club.

Franz-Josefs-Kai 29.
Tel: 533 25 75.
www.jazzland.at. Open:
from 7pm, live music from
9pm. Closed: Sun.

Kammeroper
This Jugendstil theatre
hosts finely crafted,
smaller-scale opera
productions (chamber,
Baroque and opera) as
well as contemporary
musical theatre.
Fleischmarkt 24.
Tel: 512 01 00 77.
www.wienerkammeroper.
at. Box office open:
Mon–Fri noon–6pm (on
concert days until
7.30pm), Sat 4–7.30pm
(concert days only).
U-Bahn: Schwedenplatz.

Konzerthaus
One of Vienna's most
progressive and
ambitious artistic venues.
The programme is a
mix of classical and
contemporary music
and the occasional
jazz festival.
Lothringerstrasse 2.
Tel: 242 00 2. Email:
ticket@konzerthaus.at.
www.konzerthaus.at.
Box office open: Mon–Fri
9am–7.45pm, Sat 9am–
1pm, as well as Sat, Sun
& public holidays from

45 minutes prior to the
performance. *U-Bahn:
Stadtpark; tram D.*

Kursalon

The neo-Renaissance spa
house in the city's
Stadtpark is a perfect
setting for concerts of
works by Johann Strauss.
*Johannesgasse 33.
www.kursalonwien.at and
www.strauss-konzerte.at.
U-Bahn:
Stadtpark/Stubentor;
tram 71 or D.*

Loos Bar

Also known as the
American bar, this gem
of Art Nouveau
architecture was designed
by Adolf Loos in 1908.
No photographs allowed.
*Kärntner Durchgang 10.
www.loosbar.at*

Musikverein

The 'music club' is one
of the world's leading
concert halls. The Grand
Hall holds 1,800, the
smaller Brahms-Saal
seats 600. There are 600
concerts a year, but the
Vienna Philharmonic
features in only a
handful. You can order
standing tickets up to
three weeks in advance.
*Bosendorferstrasse 12.
Tel: 505 81 90. Email:*

*tickets@musikverein.at.
www.musikverein.at.
Box office open: Mon–Fri
9am–8pm, Sat 9am–1pm.
Closed: Sun and public
holidays. U-Bahn:
Karlsplatz.*

Odeon

Classical music is just
part of what's on offer.
The theatre also plays
host to the avant-garde
Serapions Theatre
ensemble.
*Taborstrasse 10.
Tel: 216 51 27. Email:
odeon@odeon-theater.at.
www.odeon-theater.at.
U-Bahn: Schwedenplatz;
tram 1 or 2.*

Onyx Bar

The bar has a great view
from the 6th floor of St
Stephen's Cathedral.
*Located in the futuristic
Haashaus on
Stephansplatz.
Tel: 535 39 69 0.
www.doco.com. Open:
9am–2am daily. U-Bahn:
Stephansplatz.*

Passage

A cooler, smaller venue
for house, funk and
techno spun by top DJs.
Come here to dance;
there is not much
seating.
Ringstrasse/corner of

*Babenbergerstrasse.
Tel: 961 88 00.
www.sunshine.at*

Planter's

This cocktail bar is
redolent of colonial India
– thanks to the palms,
teak panelling and club
armchairs from London.
*Zelinkagasse 4.
Tel: 533 33 93.
www.plantersclub.com.
Open: 5pm–4am.
U-Bahn: Schottenring.*

Porgy and Bess

Features jazz, both
classic and experimental;
cabaret on other nights.
*Riemergasse 11.
www.porgy.at. U-Bahn:
Stubentor.*

Schlosstheater Schönbrunn

The oldest and most
ornate Viennese
auditorium, dating
from 1749.
*Schönbrunner
Schlossstrasse 47.
Tel: 0664 111 16 00.
www.musik-theater-
schoenbrunn.at. Box office
open: daily 10am–7.30pm
(Mon until 6pm).
U-Bahn: Schönbrunn.*

Staatsoper (Vienna State Opera)

Home of the Vienna
Philharmonic, one of

the world's great orchestras.
Opernring 2.
Tel: 514 44 22 50.
www.wiener-staatsoper.at.
Box office open: Mon–Fri 8am–6pm, Sat, Sun & public holidays 9am–noon, Sat during Advent 9am–5pm.
U-Bahn: Karlsplatz.

Theater an der Wien
Beethoven debuted his *Fidelio* here shortly after it opened in 1801. It offers opera all year long and is a guest theatre for the Wiener Festwochen (Vienna Festival).
Linke Wienzeile 6.
Tel: 588 30 66 0. Email: sales@theater-wien.at.
www.theater-wien.at

U4
A very popular, avant-garde dance venue.
Schönbrunner Strasse 222; www.u-4.at. Open: Mon–Sat 10pm–late.
U-Bahn: Meidlinger Hauptstrasse.

Volksgarten
One of the Vienna DJ clubs for all genres, with a huge summer garden.
Burgring 1.
www.volksgarten.at.
U-Bahn: Volkstheater.

Volksoper
Artistic standards are high and prices low, but the acoustics are not comparable to the Staatsoper or the Musikverein. The programme focuses on opera and operetta.
Währinger Strasse 78.
Tel: 514 44 36 70.
www.volksoper.at.
Box office open: Mon–Fri 8am–6pm, Sat, Sun & bank holidays 9am–noon.
U-Bahn: Währinger Strasse/Volksoper; bus 40A.

Wiener Sängerknaben (Vienna Boys' Choir)
Little boys dressed in blue and white sailors' uniforms (the Wiener Sängerknaben) began singing for the court of Maximilian I in 1498. Today, four different choirs perform 300 concerts each year.
Augartenpalais.
Tel: 216 39 42.
Email: office@wsk.at.
www.wsk.at.

WUK
A cultural and performing arts centre used for all sorts of dance parties.
Währinger Strasse 59 (near Volksoper).
www.wuk.at

SPORT AND LEISURE

Bicycle Rental Hochschaubahn
Prater 113, near the Hochschaubahn (Roller Coaster). Tel: 729 58 88. www.radverleih-hochschaubahn.com. Open: 10am until dusk. Closed: winter.

Bicycle Rental Pedal Power
Ausstellungsstrasse 3.
Tel: 729 72 34.
www.pedalpower.at.
Open: Mar, Apr & Oct 8am–6pm; May–Sept 8am–7pm.

Bicycle and Skate Rental Copa Cagrana
Bicycle delivery to hotels.
Reichsbrücke and Donauinsel, Am Damm 1.
Tel: 263 52 42.
www.fahrradverleih.at.
Closed: winter.

Bicycle and Skate Rental Ostbahnbrücke
Bicycle rental for people with disabilities. Only open during good weather.
S-Bahn Lobau station.
Tel: 0664 974 37 18.
www.radverleih-ostbahnbruecke.at

**Danube Island
(Boating and sailing)**
*www.donauinsel.at.
U-Bahn: Donauinsel/
Neue Donau.*
DDSG Blue Danube
Sightseeing trips with the
Hundertwasser riverboat
and others (MS *Schlögen,
Vinobona, Prinz Eugen).
Boats depart from
Schwedenplatz (U1).
Tel: 588 80 0. www.ddsg-
blue-danube.at. Trips
several times daily,
Apr–Oct.*
Gänsehäufel
Swimming (in the
Danube).
*Moissigasse 21.
Tel: 269 90 17.
Open: May–Sept. U-
Bahn: Kaisermühlen/
Vienna International
Centre; bus 90.*
**Old Danube
(Boating and sailing)**
*www.alte-donau.info.
U1: Alte Donau.*
Radsport Nussdorf
Bicycle delivery to hotels.
*On the Donaupromenade
at the bicycle path.
Tel: 370 45 98.
www.donau-fritzi.at*
**Tanzschule Willy
Elmayer**
Dance lessons.
Bräunerstrasse 13.

*Tel: 512 71 97.
www.elmayer.at*

WACHAU
Krems an der Donau
ACCOMMODATION
Ilkerl ★
A family-run wine estate
2.5km (1½ miles)
outside Krems. There are
six rooms including a
suite for families.
*Rehberger Hauptstrasse
57. Tel: 02732 857 58.
www.weinserver.at/ilkerl*

EATING OUT
Hofbauer ★★
Come here to pay
homage to regional
cooking that makes use
of the freshest produce
including fish, game and
forest mushrooms paired
with fruity Gruener
Veltliner or Riesling.
*Steiner Landstrasse 5.
Tel: 02732 822 61.
www.museums-
wirtshaus.at*
Jell ★★
Sample fresh fish from
the Danube or a
wonderful roast pork
accompanied by the
mineral-rich, tart wines
of the Wachau.
*Hoher Markt 8–9.
Tel: 02732 823 45.*

*Open: Tue–Sun (Sat &
Sun lunch only). Closed:
Mon.*

Melk
SPORT AND LEISURE
**Brandner Schiffahrt
(Boat trips)**
*Tel: 07433 25 90 21.
www.brandner.at*
Cruising on the Danube
Information about
cruising and where the
Danube boats stop.
www.donaustationen.at
**Donauschiffahrt
Wurm & Köck
(Boat trips)**
*Tel: 0732 78 36 07.
www.donauschiffahrt.de*
Golfclub Maria Taferl
*Tel: 0741 33 50.
www.gc-mariataferl.at*
**Golfland
Niederösterreich**
*Tel: 536 10 60 21.
www.niederoesterreich.at/
golfland*
Hagebau Schuberth
Bike rental and repair.
*Spielberger Strasse 25.
Tel: 02752 50 60.*
MS Stadt Wien
Cruises in a steamship
(*Sun; July–Aug Sat, Sun*).
*Tel: 0664 253 46 41.
www.schiff-tulln.at*
Naufahrt
Trips in historic boats.

Tel: 02752 719 47 or 0664 790 09 68 (Wolfgang Speckner).
www.naufahrt.at.tf

BURGENLAND
Eisenstadt
ACCOMMODATION
Ohr ★★
Award-winning restaurant. Good, comfortable rooms.
Ruster Strasse 51.
Tel: 02682 62 46 0.
www.hotelohr.at

EATING OUT
Haydnbräu ★
This cheap and cheerful brew pub serves up Viennese classics.
Pfarrgasse 22.
Tel: 02682 63 94 5.
www.haydnbraeu.at

SPORT AND LEISURE
Intersport Zink (Fishing)
Hauptstrasse 39.
Tel: 02682 64 15 50.

Mörbisch
ACCOMMODATION
Mörbischer Hof ★★
This pension has its own swimming pond in Neusiedl Lake.
Seestrasse 64.
Tel: 02685 80 11.
Fax: 02685 80 11 34.
www.moerbischerhof.at

Sporthotel Rust ★★
An idyllic setting on the lakeshore, with vineyards all around.
Mörbischer Strasse 1–3.
Tel: 02685 64 18.
www.drescher.at

Neusiedl am See
SPORT AND LEISURE
Sport Moser (Fishing)
Obere Hauptstrasse 30.
Tel: 02167 24 91.
Zoofachgeschäft Paar (Fishing)
Untere Hauptstrasse 63.
Tel: 02167 86 10.

Podersdorf am See
SPORT AND LEISURE
HANG ON! Kiteboarding School
Yachthafen 2/1, Jois.
Tel: 0650 7452 666.
www. hangon-kiteboarding.com
Kite2fly.com
Seeufergasse 17.
Open: Apr–Oct.
Kiteschule Kiteriders
North beach (Nordstrand).
Tel: 0699 8125 8917.
www.kiteriders.at
MissionToSurfAustria.At
South beach (Südstrand).
Tel: 0676 4072 344.
www.surf-schule.at

Wind- und Kitesurfschule Südstrand, Haider
South beach (Südstrand).
Tel: 0664 5640 091.
www.fun-and-surf.at

Weiden
EATING OUT
Zur blauen Gans ★★
Come here to eat fresh pikeperch from Neusiedl Lake or, more generally, any of the excellent regional cooking served with great local wines.
Weiden, Seepark.
Tel: 02167 75 10.
www.blaue-gans.at.
Closed: Jan–Mar.

SPORT AND LEISURE
Segelschule Kreindl (Sailing school and windsurfing)
Seebad Weiden.
Tel: 02167 79 14.
www.sail.at

SALZBURG
ACCOMMODATION
Haus Wartenberg ★★
Salzburg's Altstadt (Old Town) is a pleasant ten-minute walk from this small, rustic hotel.
Riedenburger Strasse 2.
Tel: 0662 84 84 00.
www.hauswartenberg.com

Elefant ★★★

This traditional inn, now belonging to Best Western, claims to be 700 years old. It's located in the heart of Salzburg.
Sigmund-Haffner-Gasse 4. Tel: 0662 84 33 97.
www.elefant.at

Goldener Hirsch ★★★★

An inn that has been coddling its well-heeled guests since 1465. The lobby and bathrooms are modernised; otherwise it is still traditional.
Getreidegasse 37.
Tel: 0662 80 84 0.
www.starwoodhotels.com

Schloss Mönchstein ★★★★

One of the top hotels in the city, set in a castle with its own park. The exquisite chapel is popular for weddings.
Mönchstein-Park 26.
Tel: 0662 848 55 50.
www.monchstein.at

EATING OUT

Café Tomaselli ★

This is the local bastion of *Kaffeehauskultur*, old ladies in hats, and *Jeunesse Doré*. Mozart loved their pastries.
Alter Markt 3. Tel: 0662 8444 88000.

Grünmarkt ★

The market is the best place for a quick snack or to gather provisions – bread, fruit, vegetables and sausage – smoked, grilled or steamed.
Universitätsplatz 12.
Tel: 0662 8454 570.
Open: Mon–Fri 6am–7pm, Sat 6am–1pm.

Stranz & Scio ★

This shop regales you with pastries based on recipes popular in Mozart's day – try the *Capezzoli di Venere* or 'warts of Venus'. Each one packs a punch of nougat, chocolate and cherries.
Sigmund-Haffner-Gasse 16. Tel: 0662 84 16 38.
Open: Tue–Sat 10am–8pm.

Zum Fidelen Affen ★

A brewery-tavern with a primeval atmosphere that serves great beer and a lot of calories for little money.
Priesterhausgasse 8.
Tel: 0662 87 73 61.
Closed: Sun.

m32 ★★

This restaurant in the Museum der Moderne (Modern Art Museum) has a fantastic view of the old city. It serves light regional specialities.
Mönchsberg 32. Access via the lift from Anton-Neumayr-Platz.
Tel: 0662 84 10 00.
www.m32.at.
Open: daily.

ENTERTAINMENT

The **Osterfestspiele** at Easter and **Mozart Week** in late January are other high points of a prodigious musical calendar.

Festspiele (Festival Hall)

Crouching beneath the cliff of Mönchsberg, this is the main venue for operas and operettas and the world-class Salzburger Festspiele (Salzburg International Festival).
Hofstallgasse 1.
Tel: 0662 84 25 41.
Salzburger Festspiele: late July–end Aug. Kartenbüro der Salzburger Festspiele, Postfach 140, A-5010 Salzburg.

International Mozarteum Foundation

A classical music venue.
Schwarzstrasse 26.
Tel: 0662 88 94 00.

Jazzclub Urban-Keller

Live jazz is played here.

Schallmooser Hauptstrasse 50.

Landestheater

Classical music, ballets and plays are performed here.

Schwarzstrasse 22.
Tel: 0662 8715 12222.

Marionettentheater

This delightful theatre employs marionettes that gesticulate and dance in the air to recordings of operas and ballets.

Schwarzstrasse 24.
Tel: 0662 8724 960.
www.marionetten.at.
Open: May–Sept,
Easter, Christmas &
during Mozart Week
in Jan.

Rockhouse

A rock and pop venue.

Schallmooser Hauptstrasse 46.
Tel: 0662 8849 140.
www.rockhouse.at

Schloss Hellbrunn

Concerts are performed in this leafy setting from early May until mid-September.

Fürstenweg 37.
Located 5km (3 miles)
south of the Altstadt
(Old Town).
Tel: 0662 8203 720.
www.hellbrunn.at

SPORT AND LEISURE

Ballonclub Salzburg (Ballooning)

Kendlerstrasse 90.
Tel: 0676 3162 893.
www.flyhigh.at

Golfclub Salzburg

Schlossalle 50a, 5400
Hallein. Tel: 06245 76 68 10.
www.golfclub-salzburg.at

Golf- und Country Club Schloss Klessheim

Wals bei Salzburg.
Tel: 0662 85 08 51. www.
golfclub-klessheim.com

Landesfischereiverband Salzburg (Fishing)

Reichenhallerstrasse 6.
Tel: 0662 8426 840.
www.fischereiverband.at

Paracelsus-Hallenbad (Swimming)

Auerspergstrasse 2.
Tel: 0662 88 35 44. www.
paracelsusbad.at. Open:
Mon–Fri 10am–8pm,
Sat–Sun until 7pm.

Salzburger Drachenflieger- u. Paragleiter Club (Paragliding)

General-Keyes-Strasse 15.
Tel: 0662 43 14 86.
www.paragleiter.com

Salzburger Tauchcenter (Diving)

Innsbrucker Bundestrasse 53. Tel: 0662 82 76 45.
www.tauchcenter.at

GASTEIN VALLEY AND THE GROSSGLOCKNER ROAD

Bad Gastein

ACCOMMODATION

Hotel Grüner Baum ★★

A former hunting lodge just outside town with its own chapel, kindergarten and spa, plus thermal pools.

Kötschachtal, A-5640 Bad Gastein. Tel: 0643 42 51 60. www.hoteldorf.com

SPORT AND LEISURE

Ski schools

For more information, see *www.schneesportgastein. com.* General information about ski facilities can be found at *www.schigastein.at/ index_engl.php,* and ski rental at *www.sport-fleiss.at*

Döllach

ACCOMMODATION

Nationalparkhotel and Restaurant Schlosswirt ★★

A mountain resort with swimming pool, sauna, tennis courts and a stable of Haflinger horses.
The horses are used for summer trekking and winter sleigh rides.

Hiking tours are also available.
Döllach 100, Grosskirchheim.
Tel: 0482 54 11 0.

SALZKAMMERGUT
Bad Ischl
EATING OUT
Villa Schratt ★★★
The villa built by Emperor Franz Joseph for his mistress, the actress Katharina Schratt, is now a cosy inn with an excellent restaurant.
Steinbruch 43.
Tel: 06132 27 35 35.
Closed: Tue & Wed.

SPORT AND LEISURE
General English-language portal about sports and leisure:
www.salzkammergut.at.
Information about ballooning can be found at *www.freiheit.at*, and paragliding at *www.paragleiten.net*

Gmunden
ACCOMMODATION
Seegasthof Hois'n Wirt ★★
This good-value pension, family-run, has its own beach on Lake Traun, making it popular for

sailing and windsurfing.
Traunsteinstrasse 277.
Tel: 07612 77 33 3.
www.hoisnwirt.at
Waldhotel Marienbrücke ★★
Located right on romantic Traun Lake, the hotel is popular for angling (they offer fishing lessons) and a charming place to sample fresh fish from the lake.
Marienbrücke 5.
Tel: 07612 64 01 1.
www.marienbruecke.at

EATING OUT
Landhotel Grünberg am See ★★
A family-operated hotel-restaurant on the eastern shore of Lake Traunsee with panoramic views. Strong on pairings of fish and wine.
Traunsteinstrasse 109.
Tel: 07612 77 70 0.
www.gruenberg.at

TYROL
East Tyrol
ACCOMMODATION
Camping Falken ★
The campsites are on flat meadows with shady trees with panoramic views of the Lienzer Dolomites.

In Lienz on the B100 driving in the direction of Tristacher See.
Tel: 04852 64 02 2.
www.camping-falken.com
Neuwirt ★
This family-run inn is in a building with a Baroque façade. It serves simple, substantial meals.
Virgen 34, Virgen, Virgen Valley.
Tel & fax: 04874 52 17.
Strumerhof ★★
A mountainside farmhouse worth seeking out just for its view of the Hohe Tauern mountains. The house speciality is wild game.
Hinteregg 1, Matrei.
Tel: 04875 63 10.
Hotel Traube ★★★
The top address in Lienz, where everything has class, from the rooftop indoor swimming pool to its cellar wine bar, the Traubenkeller. There are special weekend and off-season rates.
Hauptplatz 14, Lienz.
Tel: 04852 64 44 4.
www.hoteltraube.at
Rauter ★★★
This is Matrei's top hotel with an Art Deco style interior, swimming pools, bathhouse, tennis

courts and a fish pond to supply its restaurant with the 'catch of the day'.

9971 Matrei.
Tel: 04875 66 11.
www.hotel-rauter.at

Inn Valley
ACCOMMODATION
Gasthof Badl ★

The Steiner family are good-natured hosts at this solid, cosy *pension* located right on the Inn River near the *Autobahn* exit; its *Biergarten* fills up in the evening with cyclists pedalling up and downstream. Walk to Hall via a covered wooden bridge.

Innbrücke 4, Hall.
Tel: 05223 56 78 4.
www.badl.at

Böglerhof ★★

This traditional inn (*c.*1470) has been converted into a luxurious hotel with everything necessary for a hedonistic holiday (including sauna and swimming pool). The restaurant serves, arguably, the best *Speckknödel* in the land.

A-6236 Alpbach.

Tel: 05336 52 27.
www.boeglerhof.at

EATING OUT
Bauernmarkt ★

This farmers' market is held on Saturday mornings; it is the best source of local produce, *Wurst*, smoked ham and *Schnaps*.

Oberen Stadtplatz, Hall.

Innsbruck
ACCOMMODATION
Goldener Adler ★★

The city's most famous historic inn greets its guests with live zither music in the Goethe-Stube restaurant. The most popular rooms are 208 (Andreas Hofer) and 307 (Mozart).

Herzog-Friedrich-Strasse 6.
Tel: 0512 57 11 11.
www.bestwestern.at

Kapeller ★★

This hotel-restaurant is a quiet oasis located above Innsbruck near the magnificent Schloss Ambras. Its restaurant serves regional cooking paired with wines from its cellar.

Philippine-Welser-Strasse 96.

Tel: 0512 34 31 06.
www.kapeller.at

EATING OUT
Altstadtstüberl ★

One of the few Altstadt (Old Town) inns that still relies on a local clientele drawn by its *Gemütlichkeit* and good Tyrolean cooking.

Riesengasse 11–13.
Tel: 0512 58 23 47.

Café Central ★

Innsbruck's version of a Viennese coffee house where you can eat unspeakably good *Sachertorte* and read newspapers from all over Europe.

Gilmstrasse 5.
Tel: 0512 59 20 0.

Café Lichtblick ★

This trendy seventh-floor café in the new Rathaus has a panoramic view of the Alps.

Maria-Theresien-Strasse 18. Tel: 0512 56 65 50.
Closed: Sun.

Hofgartencafé ★

This place is ideal for people-watching; it is a cross between a *Biergarten* (beer garden) and café set in the former imperial garden.

In the Hofgarten.
Tel: 0512 58 99 57.
www.der-hofgarten.at
Neuböck ★
A deli where you can
stock up for a picnic.
Herzog-Friedrich-Strasse.
Speckschwemme ★
Buy your *Miniteufel* here
('little devils' – cured
salami-style sausages,
perfect for a picnic).
They sell out fast.
Stiftgasse 4.
Kapeller ★★
This hotel-restaurant is a
quiet oasis compared to
downtown Innsbruck:
perfect for people who
are passing through or
who prefer to stay above
Innsbruck near the
magnificent Schloss
Ambras. The restaurant
serves regional cooking
complemented by wines
from its cellar.
Philippine-Welser-
Strasse 96.
Tel: 0512 34 31 01.
www.kapeller.at
Sitzwohl Restaurant/
Bar ★★
A restaurant and lounge
located in an historic
school building in old
Innsbruck, with a designer
atmosphere and exquisite
cuisine. Specialities include

Ligurian bread salad with
octopus and tuna, and
lemon chicken with olive
and spinach gnocchi.
Gilm-Schule, Stadtforum.
Tel: 0512 56 28 88. www.
restaurantsitzwohl.at

ENTERTAINMENT
Landestheater
This theatre has its
own orchestra and is a
venue for opera, ballet
and drama.
Rennweg 2.
Tel: 0512 52 07 44.
www.landestheater.at
Schloss Ambras
An elegant venue for
classical concerts in
summer (*June–early*
Aug). From late May to
September, Renaissance
music is performed on
the Goldenes Dachl
balcony every Sunday at
11.30am. There is an
Accordion Festival every
three years in May (*next*
in 2010).
Schlossstrasse 20.
Tel: 0525 24 48 02.
www.khm.at/ambras

SPORT AND LEISURE
For general information,
see *www. tirol.gv.at/*
themen/sport or
www.tiscover.at

Bobsled
Tried-and-tested pilots
take passengers on the
Olympic Bobsled at
speeds of over 100kph
(60mph). The time of
the run is approximately
one minute.
Igls. Tel: 0512 37 71 60.
www.knauseder_event.at.
Open: Wed–Fri 4–6pm.

Kitzbühel
ACCOMMODATION
Camping Schwarzsee ★
This camping site is
located on a hilly
meadow at the edge
of a forest. There is a
golf course nearby.
Off the B170, 2km
(1¼ miles) outside
Kitzbühel in the
direction of Wörgl.
Tel: 05356 28 06. www.
bruggerhof-camping.at
Hotel Jägerwirt ★★
A family-run hotel
close to the town centre,
with British guests.
Jochberger Strasse 12.
Tel: 05356 69 81.
www.hotel-jaegerwirt.at
Romantik Hotel
Tennerhof ★★★
This is a self-described
'rendezvous for golfers
and gourmets' with a
view of Hahnenkamm.

Griesenauweg 26.
Tel: 05356 63 18 1;
www.tennerhof.com

Kufstein
ACCOMMODATION
Batzenhäusl ★★
This historic inn doesn't
seem touristy despite
being at the foot of the
castle. Its restaurant
serves Tyrolean dishes.
Römerhofgasse 1.
Tel: 05372 62 43 3.

EATING OUT
**Weinhaus Auracher
Löchl ★★**
You can soak in the
Gothic atmosphere
while drinking wine or
beer. Founded as a
brewery centuries ago.
Römerhofgasse 3.
Tel: 05372 62 13 8.
www.auracher-loechl.at

Lienz
ACCOMMODATION
Gribelehof ★★
Located at the edge of
the ski resort overlooking
Bruck castle, with
fabulous views of Lienz.
Luxuries include sauna
and steambath.
Schlossberg 10.
Tel: 04852 62 19 1.
www.gribelehof.com

Mayrhofen
SPORT AND LEISURE
**Ski- und Alpinschule
Mount Everest**
Peter Habeler, who,
with Reinhold Messner,
was the first man to
climb Mount Everest
without oxygen, has a
mountaineering school
that accepts beginners.
Hauptstrasse 458, Igls.
Tel: 05285 28 29.
www.habeler.com

Ötz Valley
ACCOMMODATION
**Berggasthaus
Rofenhof ★**
The highest B&B in the
Alps, run by the musical
Klotz family.
*Rofenhöfe (above the
town of Vent).*
Tel: 05254 81 03.
www.rofenhof.at
Gasthof Krone ★
This is a creaky, quaint
17th-century inn.
Dorf 6, Umhausen.
Tel: 05255 52 12.
**Ötztaler Natur
Camping ★**
Year-round camping
with mountain views on
meadows enclosed by
forest and orchards.
*Southeast of Huben
off B186. Tel: 05253 58*

*55. www.oetztaler
naturcamping.com.*
Zum Stern ★
This is a modest and
friendly guesthouse. Its
restaurant serves
gourmet Tyrolean food.
Kirchweg 6.
Tel: 05252 63 23.

Ziller Valley
ACCOMMODATION
Jägerklause ★
The owners love folk
music (they perform
some evenings) and
hunting. Wild game is
always on the menu.
Gattererberg 1a, Stumm.
Tel: 05283 27 93.
www.jaegerklause.at
Landgasthof Linde ★
The owners of this
historic inn cook with
produce from their own
garden and farm. They
organise Tyrolean
'cultural evenings' too.
Dorf 2, Stumm.
Tel: 05283 22 77.
www.landgasthof-linde.at
Landhotel Erlhof ★
A converted medieval
warehouse with its own
moorings and beach.
*Thumersbach, Erlhofweg
11, Zell am See.*
Tel: 06542 56 63 7.
www.erlhof.at

Index

Acknowledgements

Thomas Cook Publishing wishes to thank the photographer, CHRISTOPHER HOLT, for the loan of the photographs reproduced in this book, to whom the copyright in the photographs belongs (except the following):

ALLARD ZOMER 122, 123
BIGSTOCKPHOTO 10 (Steve Dunn)
DREAMSTIME 143 (Josef Muellek)
FLICKR 71 (stefan.eissing)
FOTOLIA 106 (Wilhelm Rader), 108 (Raymond Thill), 144 (Fotolibrary)
GROSSGLOCKNER 83
PICTURES COLOUR LIBRARY 77
SILBERREGION KARWENDEL 111
WIKIMEDIA COMMONS 34 (Gryffindor), 70, 127
WORLD PICTURES 1, 42, 91, 101, 115

For CAMBRIDGE PUBLISHING MANAGEMENT LTD:
Project editor: Rosalind Munro
Copy editor: Joanne Osborn
Typesetter: Trevor Double
Proofreader: Jenni Rainford
Indexer: Karolin Thomas

SEND YOUR THOUGHTS TO
BOOKS@THOMASCOOK.COM

We're committed to providing the very best up-to-date information in our travel guides and constantly strive to make them as useful as they can be. You can help us to improve future editions by letting us have your feedback. If you've made a wonderful discovery on your travels that we don't already feature, if you'd like to inform us about recent changes to anything that we do include, or if you simply want to let us know your thoughts about this guidebook and how we can make it even better – we'd love to hear from you.

Send us ideas, discoveries and recommendations today and then look out for your valuable input in the next edition of this title.

Emails to the above address, or letters to Travellers Series Editor, Thomas Cook Publishing, PO Box 227, Unit 9, Coningsby Road, Peterborough PE3 8SB, UK.

Please don't forget to let us know which title your feedback refers to!